Vegetarian

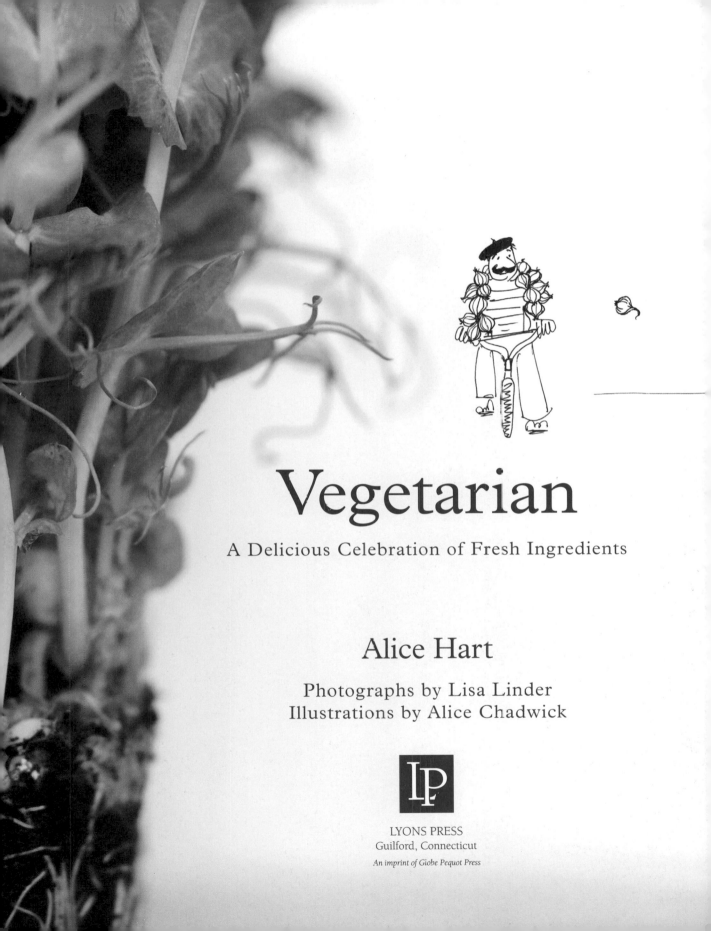

Vegetarian

A Delicious Celebration of Fresh Ingredients

Alice Hart

Photographs by Lisa Linder
Illustrations by Alice Chadwick

LYONS PRESS
Guilford, Connecticut
An imprint of Globe Pequot Press

Contents

Introduction	6
Breakfast and Brunch	20
Small Bites	38
Big Salads	72
Soups	106
Breads	128
Fast Feasts	140
One-Pots and Bakes	170
Special	202
Basics	232
Menu Ideas	246
Glossary	250
Index	252

This book is a celebration of the sublime ingredients that form the basis of a vegetarian diet.

Its purpose is to inspire even committed carnivores to eat without meat more often, and to demonstrate that meat-free cooking does not have to be worthy and dull. With a little coaxing and simple preparation, fresh and seasonal meat-free ingredients can result in dishes with deep and exciting flavors—with the added bonus that they are also nourishing.

You might not be a full-time vegetarian—you might just want to reduce the amount of meat you eat for nutritional or environmental reasons. Perhaps you feel that meat is not necessary or even practical to include in every meal. And that makes perfect sense. All too often, we view vegetables as an afterthought or a lame accompaniment to the main (meat) event. Reprising the days when vegetables, grains, legumes, herbs, and fruit were central to mealtimes makes for a joyful way to cook.

And there has never been a better time to embrace meat-free cooking; our ancestors would be astonished at the variety of produce so readily available now. It's difficult not to be inspired by tomatoes all the colors of the sunset, sweet butternut squash with skins in palettes of purple through to slate gray, and perfumeries of fragrant herbs. Meatless meals will also encourage you to explore new cuisines, new cooking methods, and new ingredients. The recipes in this book draw inspiration from around the globe, from the fragrant, spice-laden dishes of North Africa to the clean, balanced flavors of Vietnam.

One of the intentions of this book is to demonstrate that vegetarian cooking need never be boring. If you find yourself trapped in a cooking rut, as most of us do occasionally, vegetarian cooking offers a means to haul yourself out—especially if you learn to eat with the seasons.

THE VEGETARIAN COOK'S
DREAM PANTRY

Chestnuts
(vacuum-packed or cans of purée)
Dried fruit
Rolled oats
Dry yeast
Dark chocolate
Vanilla pods and extract
Rose water
Orange blossom water
Chutneys and preserves
Preserved lemons
Hot sauce
Dried sea vegetables
Jars of antipasto vegetables
Mustards
Tahini paste
Nut butters
Sugars and honeys
Maple syrup
Vinegars and wine
Oils
Whole spices
Pomegranate molasses
Olives
Capers
Miso paste
Dried mushrooms
A variety of grains and rice
Flours
Coconut
(cans of milk, cream, and flakes)
Soy sauce or tamari
Canned tomatoes
(plus tomato purée and paste)
Beans (dried and canned)
Lentils and peas (dried)
Nuts and seeds
Dried pasta and noodles
Sea salt
Peppercorns
(black, white, and Szechuan)

FOR THE FREEZER

Bread crumbs
Kaffir lime leaves
Parmesan rinds
Wonton wrappers
Pastry
Peas
Edamame beans

Achieving balance

There is evidence that vegetarians suffer lower rates of coronary heart disease, obesity, hypertension, and some other illnesses. This is because a nonmeat diet tends to be rich in carbohydrates, omega-6 fatty acids, fiber, vitamins, and minerals, and is low in saturated fat and cholesterol. It is also true that a vegetarian diet can sometimes lack protein, vitamin B12, calcium, omega-3, iron, zinc, and some other minerals. But these requirements can be met if you eat a wide variety of food that includes fruit, vegetables, leafy greens, whole grains, nuts, seeds, and legumes.

Obtaining protein

The average person should consume about 50g of protein per day, and getting this in a vegetarian diet is easy. Legumes, nuts, seeds, soy, leafy green vegetables, eggs, cheese, milk, yogurt, whole grains, and cereals are all particularly high in protein. When you can, combine legumes with whole grains, nuts, or seeds to form "complete" protein, which contains all the amino acids your body needs.

THE FOLLOWING MENU
WOULD PROVIDE YOU
WITH YOUR DAILY PROTEIN
REQUIREMENT

start

GRANOLA WITH YOGURT
(15G PROTEIN)

middle

HUMMUS WITH PITA BREAD
AND SALAD
(15G PROTEIN)

between

BLACKBERRY MILKSHAKE
(10G PROTEIN)

end

RICOTTA GNOCCHI
WITH STIR-FRIED GREENS
(15G PROTEIN)

IDEALLY, AN AVERAGE
DAILY NONMEAT
DIET SHOULD INCLUDE

three

SERVINGS OF STARCHY FOODS
LIKE GRAINS OR POTATOES

five

SERVINGS (AT LEAST) OF FRUIT
AND VEGETABLES

three

SERVINGS OF PROTEIN
LIKE BEANS, TOFU,
EGGS, NUTS, OR SEEDS

two

SERVINGS OF DAIRY
LIKE MILK, CHEESE, OR YOGURT

three

SERVINGS (MAXIMUM)
OF OIL, FAT,
OR SUGARY FOODS

Approximate protein equivalents in meat and vegetarian foods

2 large pork sausages = 1 1/4 cups red lentils = *20 grams protein*

Half a can of tuna = 3 large eggs = *18 grams protein*

6 oz Steak = 1 1/4 cups Peanuts = *47 grams protein*

Conversion charts

LENGTH				WEIGHT				LIQUID	
cm	inches	cm	inches	g	oz	g	oz	ml	fl oz
2mm	1/16	13	5	5	1/8	150	5½	30	1
3mm	1/8	14	5½	10	¼	175	6	60	2
5mm	¼	15	6	15	½	200	7	80	2¾
8mm	3/8	16	6¼	20	¾	225	8	100	3½
1	½	17	6½	30	1	250	9	125	4
1.5	5/8	18	7	35	1¼	275	9¾	160	5½
2	¾	19	7½	40	1½	300	10½	185	6
2.5	1	20	8	50	1¾	350	12	200	7
3	1¼	21	8¼	55	2	375	13	250	9
4	1½	22	8½	60	2¼	400	14	300	10½
5	2	23	9	70	2½	450	1lb	350	12
6	2½	24	9½	80	2¾	500	1lb 2oz	375	13
7	2¾	25	10	85	3	550	1lb 4oz	400	14
7.5	3	30	12	90	3¼	600	1lb 5oz	500	17
8	3¼	35	14	100	3½	700	1lb 9oz	600	21
9	3½	40	16	115	4	800	1lb 12oz	650	22½
10	4	45	17¾	120	4¼	900	2lb	700	24
11	4¼	50	20	125	4½	1kg	2lb 3oz	750	26
12	4½			140	5			800	28
								1 liter	35
								1.25	44
								1.5	52

Seasonal eating

To get the maximum taste and nutritional benefit from vegetable and freshly harvested. In other words, eat what the seasons deliver.

Spring

blood oranges, valencia oranges, peas, seville oranges, Swiss chard, spinach, bananas, cherries, strawberries, beans, kumquats, leeks, honeydew melon, cantaloupe, watermelon, lychees, grapefruit, lemons, mandarins, snow peas, sugar snap peas, broccoli, mangoes,

Summer

eggplant, apricots, green beans, bananas, lychees, passion fruit, mangoes, melons, cucumber, leeks, squash, nectarine, pineapple, tomatoes, valencia oranges, zucchini, white nectarines,

Autumn

apples, bananas, potato, pumpkin, celery, figs, turnip, grapes, guava, papaya, cantaloupe, lemons, limes, cauliflower, mandarins, mangosteen, Asian pears, brussels sprouts, passion fruit, peaches, persimmons, peppers, carrots, plums, pomegranate, squash,

Winter

apples, blood oranges, navel oranges, Asian pears, cherimoya, Jerusalem artichoke, brussels sprouts, parsnip, peas, grapefruit, kale, okra, olives, kiwifruit, lemons, pears, beet, limes, mandarins, cauliflower, persimmons, pineapple, quince, rhubarb, tangelos, and fruit, choose produce at optimum ripeness, which is locally grown

tangelos, tomatoes, artichokes, pineapple, asparagus, broad beans, cabbage, rhubarb, carrots, avocado, papaya, cucumber, lettuce, new potatoes, corn, cauliflower

asparagus, berries, cherries, currants, avocado, beans, borlotti beans, peppers, celery, lettuce, peaches, radish, snow peas, corn, carrots, peas

quinces, peas, cucumber, fennel, rhubarb, valencia oranges, eggplant, avocado, beans, beet, borlotti beans, cabbage, kiwifruit, leeks, lettuce, parsnip, mushrooms, onions, broccoli, Swiss chard, spinach, sweet potato

avocado, broccoli, carrot, celery root, celery, fennel, horseradish, kohlrabi, leek, onion, potato, sweet potato, turnip, pumpkin, Swiss chard, spinach, cabbage, rutabaga

If you've chosen the meat-free path, you're in excellent company.
The vegetarian Hall of Fame is filled with notable figures from across the
centuries, including those from the arts, science, politics, and religion.

Famous vegetarians

Brigitte Bardot

Claudia Schiffer

GANDHI

Buddha

BOB MARLEY

Paul McCartney

VOLTAIRE

PLATO

Lincoln

TWIGGY

DALAI LAMA

Drew Barrymore

CLINT EASTWOOD

BRAD PITT

TOLSTOY

Dizzy Gillespie

LEONARDO · DA · VINCI

Nathalie Baye

Stella McCartney

Paul Newman

TINA TURNER

VINCENT VAN GOGH

Essentials

Mushrooms and herbs

Use them because…

…if you're fond of meat but want to cut down, many mushrooms—notably gigantic field mushrooms—have a juicy, beefy quality that readily satisfies meat hankerings.

What to choose

Golden chanterelles, delicate enoki, shiitake, and tasty porcini are just a few examples, so celebrate the mushroom season and experiment. If culinary inspiration eludes you, just fry them in butter, garlic, and herbs and enjoy them on toast. Heaven.

Don't forget

Herbs make cooking joyful, so treat them well. Robust rosemary, sage, and bay need time to meld with companions in the pot, so add them early. The tender likes of basil, parsley, and cilantro go in at the end so their lovely oils don't dissipate.

Vegetables and fruit

The golden rule
It's easy to take these vegetarian staples for granted, but try not to. Complicated cooking and exotic varieties are not necessary, although I urge you to try the unfamiliar. Just buy seasonal, organic, and ripe—and pause for thought if you're inclined to cook on autopilot. You don't have to steam them every time.

Have you tried…
…sprinkling simple veg with toasted seeds or topping with a lump of nut butter? It takes just moments to raise a dish from dull to delicious. And get to know your ingredients better. Salad leaves have wildly different personalities that you can't appreciate if you only know them as the contents of a plastic bag.

Kitchen essential
Soulful onion and her cousin, garlic, are kingpins of the vegetarian kitchen, and come into their own cooked gently in oil or butter, slow roasted, or sweated in a pan. Pots of this sweet onion "confit" will keep in the refrigerator ready for use in other dishes, or can be gobbled on bread with strong cheese.

And another thing
Your kitchen armory is also lacking without lemon. A spritz here, a shower of zest there, can enliven, intensify, or transform all manner of sweet and savory dishes.

Culinary jewels

These delicious pods—including beans, lentils, peanuts, peas and soybeans—range from creamy white and dappled pink through to vivid red and smoky gray, like nature's own edible buttons and beads. Moreover, they're low in fat, high in protein, and rich in nutrients, especially vitamin B, iron, and calcium. You can even enjoy the sensory pleasure of running them through your fingers. What's not to like?

Easy prepping

Cooking legumes isn't onerous. Really. Lentils and dried peas need no soaking. Dried beans do, for 8–12 hours: just pour into a bowl of water before bedtime and they'll be plump and ready to cook by morning. If you forget to soak them, cover with water and boil fiercely for a few minutes and set aside for 2 hours, then cook as normal. Don't bother salting the water—it toughens the skin.

Fabulous flavor

Robust herbs and aromatic vegetables added to the cooking water will enhance any type of legume. Then mash, purée, mold into patties, or add to salads and casseroles as you wish. Slippery with flavorsome oil or flecked with herbs and spices, legumes also hold their own in the savor stakes.

Legumes

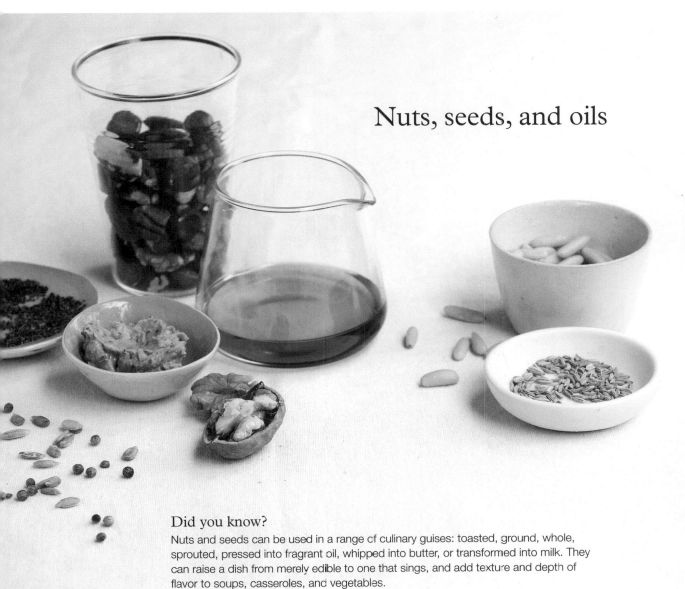

Nuts, seeds, and oils

Did you know?

Nuts and seeds can be used in a range of culinary guises: toasted, ground, whole, sprouted, pressed into fragrant oil, whipped into butter, or transformed into milk. They can raise a dish from merely edible to one that sings, and add texture and depth of flavor to soups, casseroles, and vegetables.

Noble feasting

They're tiny nutritional powerhouses: high in fiber, rich in nutrients, and an excellent source of protein. The fat in nuts is now known to be largely mono- or polyunsaturated—that's the good stuff—so they find favor with nutritionists. In any event, only modest amounts are needed to impart substance to cooking.

Why don't you try

...using rich nut and seed oils in cold food, to anoint steamed veg, or added to hot dishes at the eleventh hour so the piquancy is not destroyed by cooking. (Do give special oils a place of honor in a dark cupboard to preserve freshness.) Or, process cashews, almonds, macadamias, hazelnuts, or pecans into creamy nut butters. You can also blend various seeds to make mouth-tingling sprinkles.

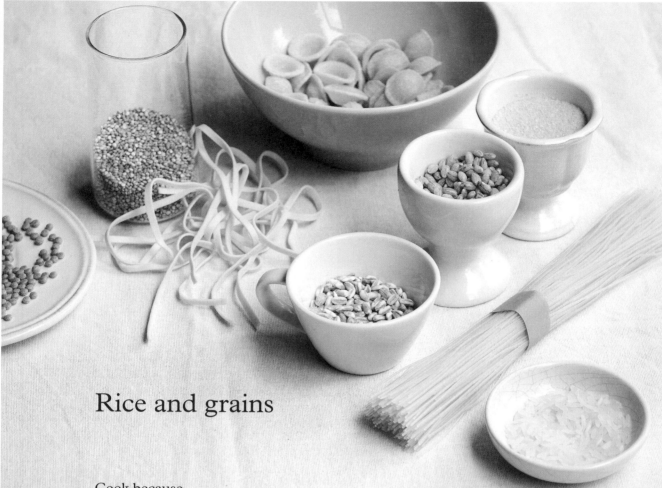

Rice and grains

Cook because...

...they are comforting, economical, delicious, and nutritious, and the starting point for countless dishes and products as varied as wine, milk, and noodles.

Which rice?

Know the basics and you can choose the most appropriate type for your purpose. Thin and dainty long-grains, cooked à point, stay separated after cooking and make fluffy beds for curries and sauces. Short- and medium-grains are plumper and starchier and stick together when cooked. Medium-grain is used in dishes like paella; short-grains makes creamy puddings and risottos.

Explore

Whole-grain rice and wild rice (a misnomer, as it's actually an unrelated grain) require more patience to cook than white rice, but the nutty, earthy flavors are worth the extra effort. Please forage in your health food shop and invite more of the unfamiliar grains into your kitchen: couscous, quinoa, amaranth, barley, bulgur...

Practical matters

Decanting rice and grain into airtight containers is not just for those who like their cupboards neat: it helps prevent them going rancid. Remember that cooked rice or grain left at room temperature can encourage bacteria to multiply, so serve when just cooked or refrigerate within 1 hour of cooking.

Dairy and eggs

Dairy treasures

Milk, butter, cream, cheese, and yogurt are the cornerstone ingredients of desserts and baking, but have a special place in vegetarian kitchens. A swirl of cream in soup, a gloss-inducing spoonful of butter in sauce, or parings of salty cheese on salad leaves: these add richness to food that might otherwise taste underwhelming. A globe of burrata or oven-baked ricotta will never leave a carnivore feeling deprived.

How about?

There are so many options. Some cheese is divine eaten raw, others are meltingly transformed by heat. Yogurt can evolve into cheese such as labne: made in a muslin mold, it emerges striated with markings and is beautiful to behold as well as eat. Some ingredients in this book, such as Parmesan, are made from animal rennet, but alternatives suitable for vegetarians are readily available, so substitute if you wish.

Naturally convenient

Eggs add substance to a nonmeat meal because they're packed with protein and are therefore filling. But they are sensitive to heat and can be tricky to cook just so. The key is not to overcook: what's the point of a luminous duck egg, served with baked sticks of celery root for dunking, if the yolk is not gooey? For the best flavor, sunniest yolks, and thickest whites, opt for free-range and organic eggs when possible.

Breakfast and Brunch

Chapter One

Almond milk has such a delicate, pure sweetness that it makes a beautiful cereal. I favor this raw, but on cold days, hot is really the only option, so heat it through gently. You can, of course, make this oatmeal with other milks in place of the almond.

Almond milk and maple oatmeal

SERVES 4
PREPARATION TIME: 10 MINUTES
PLUS SOAKING TIME
COOKING TIME: 5 MINUTES

2 cups old-fashioned oats

½ small cinnamon stick

2 cups fresh, unsweetened almond milk

¼ cup Medjool dates, pitted and chopped

½ cup sliced almonds, lightly toasted

a drizzle of maple syrup

If you can, soak the oats and cinnamon in half the almond milk the night before and keep in the refrigerator overnight. The oats will soften beautifully, enough in fact to be eaten just as they are with the dates, flaked almonds, and a little maple syrup.

Assuming you are going to cook the oatmeal, place the soaked mixture in a saucepan with the remaining almond milk. Heat gently, stirring constantly for a few minutes until the mixture turns thick and creamy. Add a little more water if it looks too thick.

Remove the cinnamon stick and divide the oatmeal between warmed bowls. Top with dates, almonds, and a drizzle of amber maple syrup.

Breakfast and Brunch

Versatile recipes such as this Aussie favorite don't like to be pigeonholed—herb- and chili-flecked baked ricotta can be breakfast, brunch, lunch, or supper. The richly sweet and smoky compote is an excellent foil for the creamy cheese.

Baked ricotta with avocado

MAKES 4
PREPARATION TIME: 15 MINUTES
COOKING TIME: 20–25 MINUTES

2 heaping cups ricotta, drained

2 tablespoons finely grated pecorino or Parmesan

1 red chili, deseeded and finely chopped

2 tablespoons chopped basil

2 eggs, lightly beaten

extra virgin olive oil, to oil and drizzle

4 thick slices sourdough bread, toasted or grilled

2 ripe avocados, halved, pitted, and sliced

1 bunch arugula

pepper compote (see page 242), to serve

Preheat the oven to 375°F (Gas 5). Beat the drained ricotta, pecorino or Parmesan, chili, basil, and eggs together and season with plenty of freshly ground black pepper and a little salt. Lightly oil four 6 fl oz (¾ cup) pudding molds or a small roasting dish and fill with the ricotta mixture. Bake for 20 minutes if using four molds or about 25 minutes if using a single roasting dish. Leave to rest for a few minutes before running a knife around the edge and turning out.

Squish the baked ricotta onto the toasted sourdough, drizzle with olive oil, and accompany with slices of avocado, arugula, and smoky sweet pepper compote.

Breakfast and Brunch

Starting this recipe the night before will result in delicious plump oats that have soaked up all the milk. You could use walnut or soy milk here instead of cow's milk and mild honey instead of the agave nectar. Or just use diluted fruit juice instead.

Pear and walnut muesli

SERVES 2
PREPARATION TIME: 10 MINUTES
PLUS SOAKING TIME

2 firm pears, cored and coarsely grated

a squeeze of lemon

1 heaping cup old-fashioned oats

2 tablespoons mixed seeds

2 tablespoons chopped walnuts

1 tablespoon agave nectar

scant ½ cup fresh pear or apple juice

scant ½ cup milk or water

plain yogurt, a few walnut halves, and fresh pear slices, to serve

The night before, toss the grated pears with the lemon juice to stop them browning and combine with the oats, seeds, and 1 tablespoon chopped walnuts in a large bowl. Add the agave nectar, pear or apple juice, and the milk or water. Stir well, cover, and refrigerate.

The following morning, stir in a rounded tablespoon of yogurt and the remaining chopped walnuts. Divide between two bowls and top with extra yogurt, walnut halves, and fresh pear slices.

Breakfast and Brunch

Delicious nut milks, seed milks, or nut-and-seed milks will last well for up to three days if kept chilled. Adding warm water and flaxseed when blending the milk helps it to emulsify evenly, making it luxuriously creamy and smooth.

How to make nut milk

nuts

rub

1/3 cup

flaxseeds

step 1.

Cover ⅓ cup of your choice of shelled nuts and/or seeds with plenty of cold water in a large bowl and leave to soak in a cool place overnight, or for at least 8 hours. The nuts and/or seeds will soften and plump up.

step 2.

If the milk is destined for a refined recipe, or if you want it to be particularly smooth, de-skin any nuts with skins remaining after their soaking time. Almonds are easy to skin by blanching—just nick with a knife and slip the white nuts out—but others such as walnuts and pecans will need to be rubbed vigorously with a clean dishtowel to remove as much skin as possible.

step 3.

Place the soaked nuts in a blender with 2 cups warm water. Add 1 tablespoon ground linseeds (flaxseed) if you have them to help the milk emulsify, but this is not essential. Blend on high speed for a couple of minutes until very smooth.

Brazil nuts, almonds, pumpkins seeds, sesame seeds, peanuts, walnuts, cashews, sunflower seeds, macadamias, hazelnuts, and pistachios are all good choices on their own or in combination, but do make sure your nuts and seeds are unroasted, and buy organic if possible.

twist   squeeze

step 5.

Finish by gathering up the cheesecloth and squeezing over the bowl to extract the liquid from the solids.

2 layers   nut milk

step 4.

Line a sieve with several layers of cheesecloth and set over a bowl. Pour the nut milk through slowly to filter out the remaining nut pieces.

dates   sugar   honey

step 6.

You can sweeten the creamy nut milk with 1–2 tablespoons (or more to taste) of maple syrup, mild honey, unrefined sugar, or a few pitted dates. To do this, return the milk to the rinsed blender, add the sweetener, and blend again. Add nothing more if the milk is to be used in savory recipes, or in smoothies or shakes, as they will be sweetened as you make them. You could also add flavorings like vanilla seeds, ground cinnamon, ground nutmeg, or cocoa powder at this stage. Dilute the milk to taste with extra water if you wish. Chill the milk or use when warm.

If you can spare 15 minutes, delicious melty panini can be yours for breakfast instead of a sad bowl of bran flakes. Wrap them in paper to keep warm for 10 minutes—this will give you just enough time to run for the bus before you sink your teeth in.

Toasted goat cheese and charred tomato panini

MAKES 2 PANINI
READY IN 15 MINUTES

2 small ciabatta rolls

1 large, ripe tomato, sliced ¼ inch thick

2½ oz soft, mild goat cheese

3 tarragon sprigs, leaves only

olive oil, for drizzling

Split each ciabatta in half horizontally. If the rolls are very thick, slice into three and save the middle section for bread crumbs, leaving you with thin top and bottom pieces.

Place a nonstick frying pan over high heat until smoking hot. Add the tomato to the pan, making sure the end pieces are cut side down. Leave undisturbed for a minute before reducing the heat to medium and leaving to char for a further minute or so. Remove from the pan with a spatula and set aside.

Beat the goat cheese and tarragon together and spread over the bottom ciabatta halves. Put the charred tomatoes onto the cheese mixture, and place the remaining ciabatta halves on top, pressing them down firmly. Drizzle the tops and bottoms of the panini with a little olive oil.

Preheat an electric sandwich press if you have one, or place a sturdy frying pan or griddle on the stove to heat. If using a sandwich press, place the panini on the ridged hotplate and press down the cover to flatten the panini as they cook. They will need at least 2 minutes, or according to your machine's instructions. If using a griddle, place the panini in the hot pan and rest a heavy frying pan on top to weigh them down. Cook over medium-high heat for a minute or two, then remove the frying pan, turn the panini over, and replace the pan to weigh them down for a further minute. Whichever way you cook them, eat while they're still warm.

The blackberry milkshake is arguably the less virtuous recipe here, but is so delicicus. Use frozen yogurt–plain, vanilla, or berry–or if your milkshake is more of a treat, replace the yogurt with a scoop of vanilla ice cream and a couple teaspoons of sugar instead of honey. Flaxseed will help the mango and cashew smoothie emulsify.

Blackberry milkshake, mango and cashew smoothie

MAKES 2 OF EACH
PREPARATION TIME: 10 MINUTES FOR EACH
PLUS SOAKING TIME FOR THE SMOOTHIE

FOR THE BLACKBERRY MILKSHAKE:

1 vanilla pod

2⅓ cups blackberries, fresh or frozen

a generous drizzle of mild runny honey

2 large scoops frozen yogurt

1⅔ cups milk, chilled

FOR THE MANGO AND CASHEW SMOOTHIE:

⅔ cup unsalted cashews

1¼ cups water, chilled

1 ripe mango, flesh chopped

1 small banana

3 ice cubes, crushed

1 tablespoon golden flaxseed

1 tablespoon old-fashioned oats

Blackberry milkshake

Split the vanilla pod along its length and scrape the seeds into a blender with the tip of the knife. (You can use the empty pod to flavor a bag of sugar in your pantry.) Add the rest of the ingredients to the blender and simply blitz together. Immediately divide between two tall glasses. That's it.

Mango and cashew smoothie

Start the evening before: soak the cashews in plenty of cold water and leave overnight to soften. The following morning, drain the cashews and place in a blender with 3½ fl oz chilled water. Blitz until a paste forms, then pour in a further 7 fl oz chilled water while the motor is running to form rich, smooth milk. This will take a couple of minutes. Throw in the remaining ingredients and blitz for at least another minute until smooth. Pour into two tall or four small glasses and drink straightaway.

Breakfast and Brunch

Make a batch of granola and you'll be set for breakfast for a couple of weeks—or you can simply snack on it from the jar. Any seasonal fruit compote will be a lovely accompaniment, but Barbie-pink rhubarb, roasted with vanilla sugar and a splash of water until tender, is perfect.

Toasted honey and pumpkin seed granola with yogurt

MAKES 12 SERVINGS
PREPARATION TIME: 10 MINUTES
COOKING TIME: 30 MINUTES

5 cups old-fashioned oats

2 tablespoons wheat germ (optional)

⅔ cup pumpkin seeds

⅓ cup sunflower seeds

⅓ cup sesame seeds

scant 1 cup shredded dried coconut (unsweetened)

scant ½ cup pumpkin seed oil or sunflower oil

⅓ cup mild, runny honey

plain yogurt, to serve

Preheat the oven to 300°F (Gas 2). Line two baking trays with parchment paper and combine all ingredients (except yogurt) in a large bowl, tossing together until evenly coated with oil and honey. Spread over the lined trays and bake for about 30 minutes, stirring the mixture at least three times to ensure everything browns evenly. The granola should be golden and smell toasted. Cool, then transfer to airtight jars. Serve in bowls with yogurt and/or milk and perhaps some fruit compote or a little fresh fruit. Or eat dry as a snack.

VARIATIONS

Apricot and almond

Use maple syrup and almond oil in place of the honey and pumpkin seed oil, and chopped almonds instead of pumpkin seeds. Replace the coconut with ¾ cup chopped dried apricots, adding them for the last 10 minutes of cooking.

Cherry and coconut

Increase the coconut to 1½ cups and use sunflower oil, not pumpkin seed oil. Add ¾ cup chopped pistachio nuts and omit the pumpkin and sunflower seeds. Add ⅔ cup dried cherries for the last 10 minutes of cooking, and serve with cherries.

Chocolate and fig

Replace the honey with light agave nectar and the seeds with 1 cup flaked almonds. Add ½ cup dried figs to the granola for the last 10 minutes of cooking. When cooled completely, stir in ⅔ cup dark chocolate, chopped small. Eat with cold milk or as it is.

Of course you can buy yogurt from the supermarket or health food shop, but there is something special about the yogurt you make yourself. Make sure you keep all your utensils scrupulously clean during this process so you don't encourage bad bacteria.

How to make yogurt

115 F   cool

2 cups   milk

add milk x 2

step 2.

Immediately set aside to cool until the temperature falls to 115°F. If you don't have a thermometer, test the temperature with a clean finger—if you can keep your finger in the milk for 10 seconds, the temperature will be about right.

step 1.

Bring 2 cups milk to a boil in a saucepan. Use whole, semi, or skimmed milk, depending on how rich you would like the finished yogurt to be.

step 3.

Discard any skin from the milk's surface and add 2 tablespoons of the milk to a small bowl containing a heaped tablespoon of live (cultured) yogurt that you have bought or made earlier.

fresh milk

Skimmed milk can be used as effectively as full-fat milk but full-fat milk will produce thicker yogurt. Whatever kind of milk you choose to use, yogurt is a healthy source of protein, calcium, magnesium, and other essential vitamins, and its active bacterial cultures aid in digestion.

warm milk mix

stir

step 5.

Pour the warm milk mix into a lidded container—a Tupperware or clean ice cream tub is ideal.

8 hours

step 6.

Place the lid on, wrap the container in a towel or blanket, and leave in a warm place for about 8 hours. You should now have a tub of yogurt! Keep chilled from this point to prevent the milk souring any further, and use within a week or so. You can use this live yogurt to make your next batch.

step 4.

Scrape the milk and yogurt mixture back into the saucepan and stir well.

Small Bites

Chapter Two

These are delicate little bites, but the cheese does lend them substance. Chard is related to beets and has an earthier taste than spinach. But if you want to, you could just use spinach leaves instead of chard here, in which case use 3 cups spinach, wilt as per the instructions for the chard, and continue with the recipe.

Chard and brie mini muffins

MAKES 12–24
PREPARATION TIME: 20 MINUTES
COOKING TIME: 15 MINUTES

2 tablespoons butter, melted, plus extra for greasing

3 cups rainbow or Swiss chard, leaves washed and shredded, stalks reserved

1¼ cups self-rising flour

2 tablespoons finely grated Parmesan

a good grating of nutmeg

⅔ cup milk

1 small egg, beaten

2½ oz brie or Camembert, cubed

Preheat the oven to 375°F (Gas 5). Grease a 12-cup standard muffin tin or a 24-cup mini-muffin tin with a little butter, or line with paper baking cups if you prefer.

Chop the chard stalks and steam for 4 minutes, add the chard leaves and steam for a further minute or so. Turn into a clean dishtowel and squeeze out any excess water.

Mix the flour, 1 tablespoon Parmesan, a pinch of salt, and the nutmeg in a bowl. In a separate bowl, beat the milk, melted butter, and egg together. Tip the milk mixture into the flour bowl and mix a couple of times. Now add the cooked chard stalks, chard leaves, and the brie or Camembert. Don't overmix or the muffins will be tough—a few lumps are just fine.

Spoon the mixture into the cups of the muffin tin, sprinkle with the remaining Parmesan, and bake for about 15 minutes until risen and golden. Cool on wire racks or eat warm.

Small Bites

Even at their best, falafel can be on the heavy side of vegetarian fare, and deep-frying them is a time-waster. Not so here. Sweet roasted squash combines beautifully with the spices and nutty chickpeas to make falafel with a lighter texture and a more rounded flavor.

Butternut squash falafel with cucumber yogurt

MAKES ABOUT 16
REPARATION TIME: 20 MINUTES
PLUS CHILLING AND STANDING TIME
COOKING TIME: 50 MINUTES

FOR THE FALAFEL:

3½ cups butternut squash, deseeded and cubed

2 tablespoons olive oil

1¾ cups cooked chickpeas, or one 14 oz can, drained

2 garlic cloves, roughly chopped

½ teaspoon baking soda

1 small bunch parsley, leaves only, chopped

1 small bunch cilantro, leaves only, chopped

1 teaspoon ground coriander

1 teaspoon ground cumin

FOR THE YOGURT:

½ cucumber, peeled, deseeded, and coarsely grated

1¼ cups thick plain yogurt

1 tablespoon lemon juice

Preheat the oven to 400°F (Gas 6). Toss the butternut squash with 1 tablespoon olive oil and season well. Spread out on a baking tray and roast for about 35 minutes until soft and caramelized. Set aside to cool.

Place the well-drained chickpeas in a food processor with the garlic, baking soda, parsley, cilantro, and cumin. Pulse the machine, stopping every now and then to scrape down the sides with a spatula, until the mixture forms a rough paste. Tip into a large bowl and season well with salt and pepper.

Crush the roasted squash with a fork until very roughly mashed and add to the chickpeas. Fold everything together. Chill for 30 minutes if you have time.

Scoop heaping teaspoonfuls onto a baking tray lined with parchment paper and space out well. Drizzle with the remaining olive oil and bake at 400°F (Gas 6) for 15–20 minutes until golden underneath.

To make the cucumber yogurt, scoop the grated cucumber into a colander or sieve, sprinkle with salt, and set aside for 20 minutes. Rinse and squeeze dry with a clean dishtowel. Stir into the yogurt with the lemon juice and some salt and pepper to taste. Serve with the falafel, adding flatbread and salad if this is more of a sit-down affair.

Black vinegar should be easy to source at Chinese food shops, but if you don't have the means or inclination, try two tablespoons of rice vinegar instead. The wonton wrappers can be a little fiddly, but it gets easier as you go along, and the results are well worth it.

Potsticker dumplings with black vinegar dipping sauce

MAKES ABOUT 36
PREPARATION TIME: 20 MINUTES
COOKING TIME: 25 MINUTES

FOR THE DIPPING SAUCE:

4 tablespoons light soy sauce

3 tablespoons black vinegar

1 teaspoon superfine sugar

2 tablespoons chili oil

FOR THE POTSTICKERS:

1⅓ cup Savoy cabbage, sliced wafer thin

3 tablespoons vegetable oil

2 garlic cloves, crushed

1½ inch piece ginger, finely chopped

1⅔ cups shiitake mushrooms, finely chopped

3 spring onions, finely sliced

3 carrots, grated

1 large bunch cilantro, finely chopped

1 teaspoon white pepper

1 tablespoon light soy sauce

1 teaspoon sesame oil

36 round wonton wrappers

Start with the dipping sauce: combine all the ingredients and set aside.

Finely chop the cabbage slices. Place 1 tablespoon vegetable oil, garlic, and ginger in a large wok and set over medium heat. Cook, stirring, for a minute until the mixture sizzles, then add the chopped cabbage, mushrooms, spring onions, and carrots. Stir-fry for 5 minutes or so until the mixture softens and any liquid in the pan evaporates.

Remove from the heat and stir in the cilantro, followed by the white pepper, soy sauce, sesame oil, and a generous pinch of salt. Allow to cool a little.

Place 2 teaspoons of this filling in the middle of a wonton wrapper and brush the border with water. Fold over to form a half-moon shape, pleating the edges together about 5 times as you go. Press the edges firmly to seal completely. Sit the dumplings so the seam is vertical and the base is flat, on a baking tray lined with parchment paper. Cover with a damp dishtowel as you make them.

Now, pour 1 tablespoon of the remaining oil into a large nonstick frying pan and set over medium heat. Add half the dumplings to the pan, flat base down. Fry them undisturbed for about 2 minutes until golden underneath. Pour ¾ cup plus 1 tablespoon of water into the pan, bring to a boil, then reduce the heat slightly. Cover with a lid or a large baking tray and simmer for about 8 minutes, or until no liquid remains in the pan. Serve straightaway with half the dipping sauce and repeat the cooking process with the remaining dumplings.

Small Bites

Panelle are traditional Italian chickpea pancakes that are made in a very similar way to firm polenta—season the batter well and get the panelle good and golden in the pan. There might be extra caponata left over, but it keeps beautifully, chilled, for up to two weeks.

Robust caponata spooned onto panelle

MAKES ABOUT 25
PREPARATION TIME: 25 MINUTES
PLUS COOLING TIME
COOKING TIME: 50 MINUTES

FOR THE CAPONATA:

2 medium vine tomatoes

2 eggplants, cubed

scant ½ cup olive oil, divided

1 red onion, finely sliced

2 celery stalks, sliced

⅓ cup green olives, pitted and halved

2 tablespoons white wine vinegar

2 tablespoons superfine sugar

2 tablespoons pine nuts, lightly toasted

FOR THE PANELLE:

4 tablespoons extra virgin olive oil

1¼ cups chickpea flour

parsley sprigs, to serve

Nick the bases of the tomatoes and cover with boiling water. Leave for a minute, then drain and peel the skin away. Chop the tomato flesh.

In a large frying pan, fry the eggplant in ⅓ cup of the olive oil, stirring until golden all over. Scoop out and set aside on a plate. Turn down the heat, add onion and 1 tablespoon olive oil to the pan, and sauté until golden. Add the celery and continue to cook for a minute, followed by the tomatoes, olives, vinegar, sugar, and pine nuts. Simmer gently for 15 minutes. Cool to room temperature and season to taste.

For the panelle, pour 1⅔ cups water into a saucepan with 1 tablespoon of the olive oil and add the chickpea flour in a steady stream, whisking as you go. Cook over medium heat, stirring constantly with a wooden spoon, until the mixture thickens—this will take longer than you think, so allow 20 minutes. Lay a piece of parchment paper on a chopping board, and spread the thickened mixture onto it; it should be just over ½ inch thick.

Leave until cool and firm, then cut into small squares or diamond shapes and fry in the remaining 1 tablespoon olive oil until golden and crisp on both sides. Spoon a little caponata onto each of the panelle, add a parsley sprig, and serve.

Small Bites

If the idea of perfect little spheres offends you, try crushing the coated cheese slightly with the back of a fork. Drizzle the bites with olive oil and offer toasted flatbreads to scoop them up.

Roasted red pepper and goat cheese bites

MAKES ABOUT 30
PREPARATION TIME: 15 MINUTES

2 roasted red peppers in olive oil, drained and chopped

1 cup firmly packed, soft goat cheese, curd cheese, or labne (see page 50)

2 tablespoons coriander seeds, toasted and crushed

1 teaspoon black pepper, crushed

4 tablespoons finely chopped cilantro

extra virgin olive oil, to cover (optional)

Stir the chopped peppers into the cheese and roll into heaped-teaspoon-sized balls.

Combine the coriander seeds, black pepper, and chopped cilantro with a pinch of salt and spread out on a large plate. Roll the cheese rounds in this mixture to coat.

Serve as they are with crisp flatbread, or if you'd rather save them for another time, place in a bowl or jar and cover with extra virgin olive oil. Chill and eat within a couple of weeks.

This cheese looks beautiful and tastes even better.
Leave to marinate for at least a day before eating
in salads or on fresh bread. It will last in its oil for up
to two weeks if you keep it chilled.

How to make labne

plain yogurt

2 cups

cheesecloth

yogurt

cloth

step 1.

Rinse and wring out several
layers of cheesecloth and
use it to line a colander or
sieve, ensuring excess cloth
overhangs the edges. Set the
colander or sieve in or over a
mixing bowl.

step 2.

Stir ½ teaspoon salt into
2 cups plain yogurt (or
3 tablespoons superfine sugar
if you would prefer a sweet
cheese). You can also add
flavorings and spices at this
stage: citrus zest, a teaspoon
of crushed coriander or cumin
seeds, a pinch of dried chili,
chopped herbs, or vanilla seeds
scraped from a pod.

step 3.

Spoon the yogurt into
the cloth and fold the
overhanging edges over.

Ingredients for your labne include: plain yogurt, salt,
superfine sugar, lemon, dried apricots,
coriander seeds, cumin seeds, dried chili,
thyme and other fresh herbs, olive oil.

superfine sugar

unwrap

15½
hours

plate

step 4.

Set a small plate on top
and weigh down with an
unopened can or bottle.
You will not need much
weight to press the yogurt.
Leave in a cool place for
up to 15 hours.

step 5.

The longer you leave
the cheese, the firmer
it will be. To speed up
the process, gently
squeeze the cheesecloth
to force extra water out
of the cheese. Carefully
unwrap the cheese and
turn onto a plate. It will
have a domed shape
with beautiful markings
from the cloth.

add olive oil,
herbs and seeds

step 6.

Use as it is or beat in extra herbs for a savory
version, or chopped dried fruit for a sweet
cheese. The drained whey can be used to
make bread, or discarded. The cheese will
keep, chilled and covered, for up to 4 days,
but you can also form it into walnut-sized balls
and place in a sterilized jar. Pour over enough
extra virgin olive oil to cover and add a few
robust herb stalks such as rosemary or thyme,
and perhaps a few coriander seeds. Leave the
cheese to marinate for at least a day before
eating in salads or on fresh bread.

Any edible squash blossoms would be perfect here, but if none are available, a delicate seasonal vegetable would be lovely, such as young, fresh asparagus. Enjoy these warm or cold.

Squash blossom and tomato frittatas

MAKES 12
PREPARATION TIME: 10 MINUTES
COOKING TIME: 15–20 MINUTES

2 tablespoons olive oil, plus extra for oiling

1 fat garlic clove, crushed

1 tablespoon butter

1¼ cups cherry tomatoes

12 squash blossoms

6 large eggs

scant ½ cup light cream

a small handful of basil leaves

Preheat the oven to 400°F (Gas 6). Oil a 12-cup nonstick muffin tin with olive oil.

Pour the 2 tablespoons olive oil into a frying pan and add the garlic. Place over low heat and cook gently, stirring, for a couple of minutes. Turn the heat up and add the butter and tomatoes. Cook for a couple of minutes, then add the squash blossoms. Cook for a brief minute to wilt them, then remove the pan from the heat.

Beat the eggs, cream, and basil together and season well. Spoon this mixture into the cups of the muffin tin, top with some of the garlicky tomato and a wilted squash blossom.

Bake for 15–20 minutes until puffed up and golden. Leave to stand for a few minutes before turning out.

This full-flavor trio is dedicated to all things mellow and earthy: roasted garlic is subtle, carrots are sweet, tahini and lentils are nutty. I serve this in bowls, with a pile of crisp toasts sitting alongside.

Puy lentil hummus, carrot and cumin hummus, garlic toasts

SERVES 4
PREPARATION TIME: 20 MINUTES
COOKING TIME: 1 HOUR 15 MINUTES

FOR THE ROASTED GARLIC TOASTS:

1 bulb garlic, unpeeled

olive oil, for drizzling

2 seeded bread rolls

FOR THE LENTIL HUMMUS:

¾ heaping cup Puy lentils, rinsed and drained

4 sun-dried tomatoes in oil

2 tablespoons chopped parsley

1 tablespoon lemon juice

FOR THE CARROT HUMMUS:

2 large carrots, sliced

2 tablespoons olive oil

1¾ cups cooked chickpeas or one 14 oz can, well drained

1 tablespoon light tahini paste

a pinch of ground cardamom

1 tablespoon lemon juice

Preheat the oven to 400°F (Gas 6). Slice the top off the garlic bulb to just expose the cloves. Drizzle with olive oil and wrap loosely in foil, sealing securely. Bake for 30 minutes or so until soft.

When cooked, squeeze the garlic cloves from the bulb into a bowl, mash with a fork, and add a good drizzle of olive oil and a pinch of salt. Cut the bread rolls into slices ¼ inch thick at most, and brush both sides with the roasted garlic mixture. Space out on a baking sheet and place in the oven for a few minutes until just turning golden at the edges.

Cover the lentils with 2 cups cold water in a saucepan and bring to a boil. Simmer gently for about 30 minutes, stirring occasionally until the liquid has been absorbed. Transfer to a blender and add a teaspoon of the roasted garlic mixture, the sun-dried tomatoes and a drizzle of their oil, parsley, and lemon juice. Blend to a rough purée, adding a little water if necessary, and season to taste with salt and pepper.

Place the carrots in a separate saucepan with enough water to cover them. Add the 2 tablespoons olive oil and a pinch of salt and bring to a boil. Simmer for about 8 minutes until the carrots are tender. Pour the whole lot into a blender with the chickpeas, tahini, cardamom, lemon juice, and a teaspoon of the roasted garlic mixture. Blend until pureed. Serve with the toasts and lentil hummus.

Serrano chilies are the longish, pointed variety commonly available in supermarkets: use red or green in the guacamole as you wish, but go easy if they are extra fiery. This dish also works well with large potatoes, and their cooking times have also been included in this recipe.

Cumin potato skins and guacamole salsa

SERVES 4
PREPARATION TIME: 20 MINUTES
COOKING TIME: 50–60 MINUTES

FOR THE POTATO SKINS:

15 new potatoes or small waxy potatoes

3 tablespoons olive oil

2 teaspoons cumin seeds

FOR THE SALSA:

½ teaspoon cumin seeds

4 large, ripe avocados, halved and pitted

2 ripe tomatoes, deseeded and diced

½ red onion, finely chopped

2 serrano chilies, deseeded and finely chopped

juice of 1 large or 2 small limes

2 tablespoons chopped cilantro

Preheat the oven to 350°F (Gas 4). Scrub the potatoes lightly if they look muddy, sprinkle with a little salt, and bake for 50–60 minutes until tender. Set aside to cool a little. Cut each potato in half and scoop out the flesh. This is perfect for turning into mashed potatoes (just beat in butter, salt, and milk to taste), for making vegetable patties, or even adding to bread dough before baking. Drizzle the potato skins with the olive oil and rub in the cumin seeds and a generous sprinkle of salt. Space out on a baking tray and bake for 15 minutes or so until crisp and golden.

Meanwhile, to make the salsa, toast the cumin seeds in a dry frying pan until fragrant. Crush roughly. Mash the avocados with a fork, but you don't want them smooth; the aim is to leave a lot of texture. Stir in the remaining ingredients, including the toasted cumin seeds, and season to taste.

Serve the crisp potato skins alongside the salsa, with a spoon for scooping, or spoon the salsa into each potato half and eat before they soften.

This recipe can be adapted for large potatoes: just bake 4 potatoes for 1 hour 20 minutes, then halve, scoop out the flesh, and cut the skin into strips before serving with the salsa.

These dear little sizzling pancakes are close cousins of the much larger banh xec of southern Vietnam. They originate from Hue in central Vietnam and would ordinarily contain some meat or seafood, but mushrooms make a fine substitute. It's great finger food.

Mushroom banh khoai

MAKES ABOUT 18
PREPARATION TIME: 20 MINUTES
COOKING TIME: 25 MINUTES
PLUS 3–4 MINUTES PER PANCAKE

¼ cup dried mung beans

1½ cups rice flour

½ teaspoon ground turmeric

2 eggs, beaten

1 tablespoon superfine sugar

1¾ cups mixed exotic mushrooms (such as oyster, enoki, and shiitake), torn if large

1 fat garlic clove, finely chopped

vegetable oil, for frying

1¾ cups bean sprouts

2 spring onions, sliced

TO SERVE:

soft lettuce leaves and/or rice paper rounds

soft herbs

sliced cucumber

ginger and lime dipping sauce (see page 244)

Soak the mung beans in plenty of cold water for at least 30 minutes, or overnight if that's easier. Drain, then steam the beans over simmering water for 15–20 minutes until tender.

Meanwhile, mix the flour and turmeric in a bowl and gradually whisk in 1⅓ cups cold water, then the beaten eggs, sugar, and a large pinch of salt. Set aside for 10 minutes so the flour can expand and thicken the batter slightly.

Stir-fry the mushrooms and garlic in a little oil over very high heat for a couple of minutes. Season with salt and pepper and set aside.

For each pancake, place a 4½ inch blini pan or mini frying pan over medium-high heat and add a tablespoon of vegetable oil. The pan should be hot before you add just enough batter to coat the base—it should sizzle. Scatter with a few steamed mung beans, a spoonful of the cooked mushrooms, a few bean sprouts, and a few spring onion slices. Fry for a couple of minutes until the edges and base are crisp. Fold the pancake in half with a spatula and slide out of the pan. Wrap the cooked banh khoai in lettuce leaves or rice paper and dunk in the dipping sauce between bites. Serve hot with the herb leaves and cucumber.

Don't be scared off by the prospect of sprouting the chickpeas yourself before making this lovely dish. The process is really very easy, and the sprouts will be ready to use within a few days. The bonus is that they're nutritious as well as tasty.

Sprouted chickpea and avocado hummus

SERVES 4
PREPARATION TIME: 10 MINUTES
PLUS SOAKING AND SPROUTING TIME

1½ cups dried chickpeas

2 tablespoons light tahini paste

1 garlic clove, crushed

1 teaspoon sea salt

juice of 1 lime

1 ripe avocado, halved, pitted and chopped

a little paprika and avocado oil, to finish (optional)

vegetable crudités and warm flatbread, to serve

Soak the chickpeas in plenty of cold water for 12–48 hours. Leave them out of direct sunlight in a cool place. Drain the chickpeas and rinse well. Spread out on a tray or large plate and stand in a cool place (again out of direct sunlight) for 2 or 3 days while they sprout. Rinse them with cold water and drain well at least twice a day to stop them going moldy.

Bring a large saucepan of water to a boil and plunge the sprouted chickpeas into the pan. Remove from the heat, leave for a minute, then drain in a colander and refresh the sprouts under cold running water to take away any bitterness.

Place the drained sprouts in a food processor or blender with the tahini, garlic, salt, lime, avocado, and ⅓ cup - ¾ cup water, as needed, to make a smooth paste. You will need to blend the hummus for 3–4 minutes, scraping down the sides with a spatula every now and then, until it is velvety smooth.

Scoop the hummus into a serving bowl and top it, if desired, with a drizzle of avocado oil and a sprinkling of paprika.

Serve with crisp vegetable crudités and plenty of warm flatbread for scooping.

This is a truly beautiful starter or picnic recipe—it's light and incredibly pretty. If you can make it a couple of days ahead and leave the terrine mold weighed down, the flavors will mellow and it will slice like a dream. Serve with toasted flatbread.

Sunblush terrine

SERVES 4
PREPARATION TIME: 25 MINUTES
PLUS PRESSING AND CHILLING TIME
COOKING TIME: 25 MINUTES

4 red peppers, halved and deseeded

2 yellow peppers, halved and deseeded

2 orange peppers, halved and deseeded

olive oil, for roasting

2 zucchini, very finely sliced lengthwise

1 teaspoon fennel seeds, lightly crushed

a bunch of spring onions

1¾ oz sunblush (semi-dried) or sun-dried tomatoes, drained and roughly chopped

2 heaping cups ricotta

2 tablespoons snipped fennel fronds or dill

½ garlic clove, crushed

wild arugula (optional), to serve

Preheat the oven to 425°F (Gas 7). Cut the peppers into quarters and toss with a little olive oil. Spread out on a large oiled baking tray, skin sides up. Roast for 20 minutes or so until the peppers are soft and blackened. Tip into a bowl, cover with a plate and set aside while the steam loosens the skins.

Meanwhile, heat a barbecue hot plate until smoking. Toss the zucchini in a bowl with a little olive oil and the fennel seeds, and season with salt and pepper. Grill the slices in batches—they should be spread out in a single layer—for a minute or less on each side, until marked and just soft. Remove to a plate.

Now toss the spring onions in a little olive oil, season, and grill for a couple of minutes, turning with tongs, until soft and a little blackened on all sides.

Once the peppers have cooled, slip their skins off. Combine the tomatoes with the ricotta, snipped fennel or dill, and garlic. Season well with salt and pepper.

Line a 4¼ x 9½ inch terrine mold with plastic wrap, and line this with the zucchini strips, overlapping them so they completely cover the sides and base. Leave any extra overhanging the edges. Put one-third of the peppers in the base of the terrine mold and cover these with half the ricotta mixture. Pack the spring onions lengthwise on top and add half the remaining peppers, then the rest of the ricotta. Finish with the last of the peppers. Fold over any overhanging zucchini, cover with the plastic wrap, and weigh down with a couple of unopened cans. Chill for at least 5 hours, or leave overnight if you can. Turn out, unwrap, and slice. Serve with wild arugula (if using).

Small Bites

The dense and salty feta is tempered with creamy fromage frais and balanced by the honey-sweet pumpkin. The spicy harissa paste—a hot North African sauce—adds a touch of fire to these crisp tarts.

Spiced pumpkin and feta puff pastry tarts

SERVES 4
PREPARATION TIME: 20 MINUTES
COOKING TIME: 35–40 MINUTES

1 lb fresh pumpkin, deseeded and sliced

1 tablespoon olive oil

3½ oz feta

1 tablespoon harissa

1 egg, beaten

2 tablespoons fromage frais (or low-fat cream cheese)

a little flour, for dusting

14 oz all-butter puff pastry

4 thyme sprigs, leaves stripped

Preheat the oven to 400°F (Gas 6). Toss the pumpkin with the olive oil, season with salt and pepper, and spread out on a roasting tray. Cook for about 25 minutes until tender. Set aside to cool a little. Reduce the oven temperature to 375°F (Gas 5).

Cut half the feta into small cubes and crumble the rest. Beat the harissa, egg, fromage frais, and crumbled feta together in a bowl and season with pepper and just a little salt (the cheese is already salty).

Lightly flour a work surface and roll out the pastry until it's about 8 x 12 inches. Trim with a sharp knife so the sides are straight, and cut into 12 equal-sized rectangles. Space out on a baking tray. Spoon a little of the harissa mixture on the center of each piece of pastry and top with pumpkin and feta cubes. Sprinkle with the thyme and bake for 15–20 minutes until puffed and golden. Serve warm, or cool the tarts on a wire rack.

To make a fresh chutney to go with the pakora, blend a large handful of chopped mint with a small handful of chopped cilantro. Chop a small red onion and a couple of green chilies and add to the herbs with a squeeze of lime, a generous splash of water, and a pinch of salt.

Spring vegetable pakoras

MAKES ABOUT 20
PREPARATION TIME: 20 MINUTES
COOKING TIME: 2–3 MINUTES

½ teaspoon cumin seeds, crushed

½ teaspoon coriander seeds, crushed

½ teaspoon ground turmeric

½ teaspoon chili powder

½ teaspoon salt

¼ teaspoon baking powder

1⅔ cups gram or chickpea flour

4 cups vegetable oil, for deep-frying

½ lb purple sprouting or tenderstem broccoli, roughly chopped

⅔ cup shelled peas

5 spring onions, roughly chopped

Mix the cumin, coriander, turmeric, chili powder, salt, baking powder, and gram flour together in a large bowl and gradually whisk in ¾ cup plus 1 tablespoon of cold water to form a batter.

Heat the oil in a deep saucepan or wok until it reaches 350°F (Gas 4). If you don't have a thermometer, drop a little batter into the pan—it should sizzle and dance immediately if hot enough.

Add the broccoli, peas, and spring onions to the batter and stir to coat. Drop tablespoons of this mixture into the hot oil, being careful not to overcrowd the pan. Deep-fry for 2–3 minutes until golden brown. Lift out with a slotted spoon and drain on paper towels. Serve immediately, perhaps with the fresh chutney described above.

Preparing this dish is just so simple, and the real boon is that only three ingredients are needed for the terrine. It's sublime served with mayonnaise, but the terrine also works well with a basic vinaigrette.

Pressed leek terrine and Dijon mayonnaise

SERVES 8
PREPARATION TIME: 20 MINUTES
PLUS PRESSING AND CHILLING TIME
COOKING TIME: 10–12 MINUTES

3 lb young, slender leeks

½ small bunch chives, finely chopped

4 oz fromage blanc or curd cheese

FOR THE DIJON MAYONNAISE:

4 tablespoons mayonnaise (see page 236) or quality bought mayonnaise

1 teaspoon Dijon mustard

Line a standard terrine mold or 8 cup loaf pan with plastic wrap. Trim the leeks to roughly the same length as the terrine mold, leaving a little green at the ends. Rinse them well under cold running water to wash away any grit. Drop into a large pan of salted, boiling water and simmer for 10–12 minutes until completely tender to the point of a knife. Drain and leave to cool slightly.

Sprinkle the base of the terrine mold with a teaspoon of chopped chives then cover with leeks, laying them lengthwise and alternating white and green ends. Cover with a few evenly spaced teaspoonfuls of cheese. Season well with pepper, a little salt, and more chopped chives. Keep layering until all the ingredients have been used, finishing with a snug layer of leeks. Cover with plastic wrap and weigh down with a couple of unopened cans. Chill for at least 4 hours or preferably overnight. Combine the mayonnaise and mustard.

Using a sharp, serrated knife, slice the terrine very carefully and transfer to serving plates. You should get at least eight slices from one terrine. Serve with the Dijon mayonnaise.

Do make sure the oil is hot enough before you start frying these tasty vegetable morsels. The tempura should be crisp and light, never greasy, so tepid oil just won't do at all.

Mixed vegetable tempura with ponzu dipping sauce

SERVES 4
PREPARATION TIME: 15 MINUTES
COOKING TIME: ABOUT 2 MINUTES

FOR THE PONZU DIPPING SAUCE:

scant ½ cup soy sauce

2 tablespoons rice wine vinegar

1¼ inch piece ginger, finely grated

2 tablespoons lime juice

2 tablespoons orange juice

FOR THE TEMPURA BATTER:

2 egg yolks

1⅓ cups iced water

2 teaspoons cornflour

1⅓ cups self-rising flour

FOR THE REST:

4 cups vegetable oil, for deep-frying

12 asparagus spears

12 purple sprouting broccoli spears

6 baby eggplants, halved

1 red pepper, deseeded and sliced

5½ oz mixed oyster and enoki mushrooms, torn if large

Start by mixing all the ingredients together to make the ponzu dipping sauce and set aside.

To make the batter, use chopsticks or a fork to beat the egg yolks and water together. Stir in the flours quickly to keep the batter light, and don't worry about any lumps—they won't matter at all.

Pour the oil into a large wok or deep saucepan and heat to 325°F (Gas 3). If you don't have a thermometer, drop a little batter into the pan—it should sizzle immediately if hot enough. Have a large plate lined with paper towels ready. Use chopsticks or tongs to dip the vegetables, one by one, into the batter to coat, then lower straight into the oil. Cook for a minute or two until light golden all over. Be careful not to overcrowd the pan, or the temperature of the oil will drop; it's better to cook the tempura in batches. Remove with a slotted spoon and drain on the plate lined with paper towels when done.

Serve straightaway with dishes of the ponzu dipping sauce.

Small Bites

Big Salads

Chapter Three

This is a beautiful and gossamer-fine salad, more suited to a role as a starter than a main course. It's incredibly lovely but not quite substantial enough to call itself a main meal.

Shaved salad with toasted seeds

SERVES 4
PREPARATION TIME: 25 MINUTES

FOR THE DRESSING:

2 tablespoons cider vinegar

5 tablespoons extra virgin olive oil

1 teaspoon fennel seeds

a small handful of fennel fronds, roughly chopped

FOR THE REST:

2 medium beets with leaves, scrubbed but not peeled

2 small fennel bulbs, halved

½ rhubarb stalk

1 red apple, quartered and cored

2 heads Belgian endive, shredded

3 tablespoons mixed seeds, toasted

Start with the dressing: combine all the ingredients and season well.

Trim the leaves from the beet and reserve.

Use a mandoline slicer, a sharp knife, or even a vegetable peeler to pare the beet, fennel bulbs, rhubarb, and apple into fine strips or slices. Place in a bowl and add the beet leaves and shredded endive. Toss with the dressing.

Divide between serving plates and scatter each serving with a couple of teaspoons of toasted seeds.

Describing this recipe as a salad might be pushing the definition slightly, but it does contain a dressing and green leaves! Mujadhara, a traditional Middle Eastern dish, is a delicious combination of golden onions, lentils, and rice—I use brown basmati for its character.

Warm salad of slow-roasted tomatoes, labne, and almonds, on mujadhara

SERVES 4
PREPARATION TIME: 20 MINUTES
COOKING TIME: 1 HOUR

FOR THE MUJADHARA:

2 tablespoons olive oil

1 large onion, sliced

1¼ cups brown lentils

¾ cup brown basmati rice

FOR THE REST:

a pinch of saffron threads

2 tablespoons sherry vinegar

3 tablespoons olive oil

1 large bunch flat-leaf parsley, leaves only

1 cup baby spinach leaves

12 slow-roasted tomato halves (see page 242)

½ heaping cup labne (see page 50) or curd cheese

3 tablespoons sliced almonds, lightly toasted

For the mujadhara, warm the olive oil in a large saucepan, add the sliced onion with a generous pinch of salt, and soften over a low heat for 20 minutes. Turn up the heat and fry for 10 minutes more until the onion is deeply golden. Add the lentils and cover with 2⅓ cups water. Bring to a boil, cover, and simmer gently for 10 minutes. Stir in the rice, re-cover, and simmer for 20 minutes more. Remove from the heat and leave to steam for 10 minutes.

Meanwhile, soak the saffron in a couple of tablespoons of boiling water for 5 minutes. Add the vinegar and olive oil to make a dressing, and season with salt and pepper.

Combine the parsley (reserving a small handful), spinach, and the mujadhara. Pile into a serving bowl and top with the tomatoes, scoops of labne or curd cheese, sliced almonds, the remaining parsley (roughly chopped), and the dressing. Serve warm or at room temperature.

This is a deeply gratifying dish for chilly months—it offers the fresh and lively flavors of a salad, but the comfort of a more substantial meal. Keep an eye on the nuts after adding them to the roasted carrots and shallots—they're all too easy to scorch.

A winter salad

SERVES 4
PREPARATION TIME: 20 MINUTES
COOKING TIME: 35 MINUTES

16 Dutch carrots (or 1 lb baby carrots)

6 shallots, halved

¼ cup olive oil

1¼ cups walnuts, roughly chopped

⅔ cup prunes, pitted and halved

1 cup faro or spelt

2 tablespoons sherry vinegar

½ garlic clove, crushed

1 teaspoon Dijon mustard

1 small bunch flat-leaf parsley, leaves chopped

6 oz goat cheese

Preheat the oven to 375°F (Gas 5). Halve or thickly slice the carrots, depending on their size, and toss with the shallots, 2 tablespoons of the olive oil, and plenty of salt and pepper. Spread out on a baking tray and roast for about 25 minutes until caramelized and soft. Add the walnuts and prunes to the tray, sprinkling them evenly over the veg, and return to the oven to toast for a further 5–10 minutes.

Meanwhile, cover the faro with 2 cups cold water in a saucepan. Add a generous pinch of salt and bring to a boil. Cover and reduce the heat, leaving the faro to simmer merrily for 25 minutes.

When this is done, drain off any remaining water, then cover the pan and set the faro aside.

Make the dressing by whisking the remaining olive oil, vinegar, crushed garlic, and mustard together with a little salt and pepper. It should be slightly sharp to counter the sweet carrots and prunes. Combine the faro, roasted carrot mixture, half the parsley, and half the dressing in a serving bowl. Crumble the cheese over the faro and vegetables, drizzle with the remaining dressing, and scatter with the rest of the parsley.

This warm salad bursts with the sweet tastes of North Africa, and the extra large couscous grains absorb all the delicious flavors. It's a breeze to make the charmoula dressing recipe on page 244—this versatile seasoning is always handy to have on standby in the refrigerator.

Giant couscous salad with preserved lemon and charmoula

SERVES 4
PREPARATION TIME: 25 MINUTES
COOKING TIME: 50 MINUTES

4 young parsnips

3 red peppers, deseeded and sliced

3 tablespoons olive oil

2 tablespoons honey

2 preserved lemons, quartered

1 cup Israeli or giant couscous

1 quantity charmoula dressing (see page 244)

juice of 1 lemon

1 small bunch cilantro, leaves only

¾ cup Greek yogurt

Preheat the oven to 400°F (Gas 6). Slice the parsnips lengthwise into halves or quarters depending on their size. Place in a roasting pan with the peppers and coat with half the olive oil and honey. Season well and roast for about 35 minutes until caramelized. Slice the flesh from the preserved lemon quarters and discard. Cut the peel into strips.

Heat the remaining olive oil in a large saucepan, add the couscous, and stir over medium heat until golden—this will only take 4 minutes or so. Pour in ¾ cup plus 1 tablespoon of boiling water and simmer gently for about 10 minutes until the water has been absorbed and the couscous is tender.

Combine the roasted parsnips and peppers with the couscous, and add 1 tablespoon charmoula, the preserved lemon peel, lemon juice, and most of the cilantro.

Ripple the remaining charmoula through the yogurt and serve spooned onto the salad with the rest of the cilantro.

When blood oranges come into season, celebrate them with this salad. The contrasting colors of the snow-white cheese, purple leaves, and deep red fruit look glorious, and taste it, too. It's best eaten as fresh as possible, so make it at the very last minute.

Blood orange, mozzarella, toasted sourdough, and radicchio salad

SERVES 4
PREPARATION TIME: 15 MINUTES
COOKING TIME: 15 MINUTES

3 thick slices sourdough bread

a little olive oil

3 blood oranges

2 tablespoons red wine vinegar

¼ cup extra virgin olive oil

1 medium head radicchio, trimmed

a handful of wild arugula

2 balls buffalo mozzarella,
torn into pieces

Preheat the oven to 350°F (Gas 4). Tear the bread into rough pieces—they should be about the size of a small egg—and coat with the olive oil. Spread out on a baking tray and bake for about 15 minutes, shaking and stirring halfway, until golden and crisp. Set aside.

Meanwhile, place the oranges in a shallow dish—you want to catch all the juice—and cut off the tops and bottoms to expose the flesh, then carefully pare the skin away from the sides, following the curve of the fruit. Slice horizontally into disks. Measure 4 tablespoons of the collected juice into a separate bowl, and into this whisk the vinegar and olive oil. Season with salt and pepper.

Tear the radicchio into large pieces and add to the arugula in a large bowl. Throw in the toasted bread, blood oranges, and mozzarella. Drizzle with the dressing and toss very gently. Serve straightaway.

 Big Salads

The choice is yours here: toss all the ingredients together to make a vibrant salad or, if you prefer daintier bites, wrap avocado slices around the addictive pickles to make fun appetizers or canapés.

Salad of avocado with white radish and carrot pickle and satay dressing

SERVES 4 AS A STARTER
PREPARATION TIME: 25 MINUTES
PLUS PICKLING TIME

FOR THE SALAD OR WRAPS:

1 large carrot

4½ inch piece white radish (mooli or daikon), peeled

3 tablespoons white wine vinegar

2 tablespoons superfine sugar

4 ripe but firm avocados

juice of ½ lime

a small handful of cilantro or alfalfa sprouts

FOR THE DRESSING:

1 tablespoon sesame oil

2 tablespoons peanuts, toasted and finely chopped

1 tablespoon soy sauce

1 tablespoon superfine sugar

1¼ inch piece ginger, finely chopped

1 red chili, deseeded and very finely chopped

finely grated zest and juice of 1 lime

To make the pickle, cut the carrot and radishes in half crosswise and lengthwise, and slice into fine shreds. Place in a nonmetallic bowl with the vinegar, sugar, and 2 tablespoons water. Cover and set aside for at least 20 minutes or chill for up to 2 days.

Make the dressing by combining all the ingredients in a small bowl.

Halve the avocados and remove the pits. Score the skin from top to bottom with a sharp knife and peel it away carefully. Use a swivel peeler to shave the avocado into long, wide strips. Sprinkle with a little lime juice to prevent them turning brown. Chop any remaining avocado into fine dice.

If you're making a salad, gently toss the salad ingredients together, including the pickle, and spoon a little dressing over to serve. Offer the rest of the dressing alongside.

If you'd rather make little salad wraps, drain the pickle (you can use the liquid to make another batch) and add the cilantro or alfalfa sprouts and diced avocado. Lay the avocado slices out flat and place a spoonful of the pickle and salad mixture at one end. Roll up tightly. Spoon the dressing over and serve straightaway.

Orzo, a rice-shaped pasta, is what makes this salad work so well. Cook until al dente, then quickly drain and soak with the simple dressing. The hot orzo will absorb the flavors beautifully and be ready to serve straightaway. It's also fabulous eaten cold.

Artichoke, orzo, and fava bean salad with shaved pecorino

SERVES 4
PREPARATION TIME: 20 MINUTES
COOKING TIME: 25 MINUTES

12 fresh young globe artichokes or 12 whole marinated artichoke hearts

a few lemon slices and a squeeze of lemon (optional)

12 oz dried orzo pasta

1 heaping cup fava beans, pods and skins removed

finely grated zest and juice of 1 lemon

4 tablespoons olive oil

4 lemon thyme sprigs, leaves stripped

2½ oz pecorino sardo

If you're going the long way round and using fresh artichokes, fill a bowl with cold water and add a few lemon slices and a squeeze of lemon. This is to stop the trimmed artichokes turning black.

Cut off the tough tops of the artichoke leaves, then use a small knife to pare off the tough outer leaves, and remove most of the stalks. Drop each finished artichoke into the bowl of water as you work. When done, drain and transfer to a saucepan, cover with fresh water, add a squeeze of lemon, and bring to a boil. Simmer for 25 minutes or so until just tender. Drain, then cut each artichoke heart into quarters. If you're using deli-style marinated artichoke hearts, simply cut each one into quarters.

Bring a large saucepan of water to a boil, add a hefty pinch of salt and tip in the orzo. Cook until al dente, adding the shelled and skinned fava beans for the last 2 minutes of cooking. Drain the pasta and beans, transfer to a bowl, and while still warm, dress with the lemon zest, lemon juice, olive oil, lemon thyme, and salt and pepper.

Use a vegetable peeler to pare shavings of pecorino over the orzo and verdant fava beans, and gently fold through the artichoke hearts.

Quinoa is not actually a grain but a member of the beet, spinach, and chard family. It is, however, cooked in a very similar way to most other whole grains. Here it is simmered to tenderness in a mushroom-spiked stock. When cooked, each grain will unfurl like a stretched coil.

Quinoa with parsley pesto, cranberries, toasted hazelnuts, and mushrooms

SERVES 4
PREPARATION TIME: 25 MINUTES
COOKING TIME: 25 MINUTES

½ oz dried mushrooms (porcini, for example)

2 tablespoons butter

1 tablespoon olive oil

9 oz mixed fresh mushrooms, sliced if large

2 shallots, finely chopped

1 garlic clove, finely chopped

¾ heaping cup quinoa

⅔ cup dried cranberries

1 quantity parsley pesto (see page 238) made with hazelnuts instead of almonds

a squeeze of lemon

½ cup hazelnuts, toasted and roughly chopped

Place the dried mushrooms in a heatproof measuring jug and add enough just-boiled water to reach the 1⅓ cups mark. Set aside.

Melt half the butter with the olive oil in a deep frying pan. Keep the heat high and fry the mixed fresh mushrooms briskly for a couple of minutes, stirring until they are golden. Tip into a bowl and set aside. Return the pan to a slightly more gentle heat. Add the remaining butter and the shallots to the pan and cook for a few minutes until softened. Add the garlic and quinoa and cook, stirring, for about 5 minutes until the quinoa takes on a pale golden color.

Strain the soaked mushrooms through a sieve, reserving the water, and roughly chop, then add them to the quinoa. Pour in the strained mushroom water and bring to a boil. Throw in a good pinch of salt, then lower the heat and simmer gently for 18–20 minutes until the quinoa is soft and the liquid is absorbed. Fold in the cranberries and reserved browned mushrooms and set aside.

Stir a couple of tablespoons of pesto through the salad, plus a squeeze of lemon. Spoon a little more pesto over the salad and sprinkle with hazelnuts. Best served warm.

This is guacamole—but not as you know it. In an elegant twist on the traditional dip, this dish is much more of a proper meal than a snack, and sufficient ingredients are included here for four main courses: even the tortilla chips. Feel free, however, to eat it with your fingers.

Guacamole salad

SERVES 4
PREPARATION TIME: 20 MINUTES
PLUS MACERATING TIME
COOKING TIME: ABOUT 15 MINUTES

2 garlic cloves, crushed

finely grated zest and juice of 2 limes

4 tablespoons olive oil

3 wheat flour or corn tortillas

1 small red onion, halved and very finely sliced

1 teaspoon cumin seeds, toasted in a dry pan

3 large avocados, halved and pitted

2 heads red endive or radicchio

5 spring onions, finely sliced

1 small bunch cilantro, leaves only

Preheat the oven to 350°F (Gas 4). Mix the crushed garlic with the lime zest and olive oil, season with salt and pepper and brush a little of this mixture lightly over both sides of the tortillas. Slice each tortilla into 8 wedges and space out on a baking tray lined with parchment paper. Cook for 12–15 minutes, turning halfway, until crisp and golden. Set aside to cool. The tortilla chips will keep for a few days in an airtight container.

Squeeze the lime juice over the red onion and set aside for 10 minutes to macerate. Add the remaining garlicky oil to the onions and stir in the toasted cumin seeds.

Slice the avocados and combine with the remaining ingredients, including the toasted tortillas, and serve before they soften.

To sprout small seeds like alfalfa or mustard, use 2–3 tablespoons at a time. For the larger mung beans, wheat berries, and lentils, start with 2½ oz. And for the still larger likes of peas, almonds, and chickpeas, use about 7 oz per jar.

How to grow sprouts

muslin

soak seeds 4-8 hours

drain

step 1.

Soak your chosen seeds or nuts for 4–8 hours in plenty of cold water. A large, wide glass jar is ideal for this, but if you have a specially designed sprouter, follow the instructions on the box.

step 2.

Secure a piece of loose-weave muslin or cheesecloth, or cut-up tights, firmly over the opening of the jar with a rubber band. This will allow the air to circulate; a close-weave material will not breathe and will encourage mold.

step 3.

Invert the jar and drain the water away. The seeds should now be spread out along the inside of the jar.

A wide variety of nuts, seeds, and legumes are perfect for sprouting, including peas, almonds, mung beans, hazelnuts, chickpeas, and sunflower seeds.

rinse

× 2 daily

ready to eat 3–8 days

leave 45°

step 5.

Rinse the jar out with clean, cold water twice a day and return it to its angled position with the material or tights re-secured. This will stop the sprouts from growing moldy.

step 4.

Prop the jar with the opening facing down at a 45-degree angle, with a bowl or tray underneath to catch any water that drips out. Leave in a cool place, out of direct sunlight.

step 6.

Different nuts, seeds, and legumes sprout at different times, but shoots will start to grow within a couple of days, and the sprouts should be ready to eat in 3–8 days, depending on the variety and how long you want the sprouts to be. Do keep rinsing and swirling them with cold water twice every day to keep them fresh as they grow. Refrigerate finished sprouts whenever you like the look and taste of them. They are now ready to add to salads, juices, soups, sandwiches, or hummus or to eat as they are.

Cherry tomatoes come in a rainbow of colors and a range of shapes and sizes: orange, yellow, black, red, round, oval, and teardrop. A selection looks stunning atop this verdant tabbouleh.

Green tabbouleh topped with a cherry tomato salad

SERVES 4
PREP TIME: 15 MINUTES
PLUS SOAKING TIME

¾ heaping cup bulgur wheat

2 large bunches flat-leaf parsley, leaves only

1 large bunch mint, leaves only

½ cucumber, peeled, deseeded, and very finely diced

1 bunch spring onions, finely sliced

juice of 2 lemons

¼ cup olive oil

2 cups cherry tomatoes, halved if large

Cover the bulgur wheat generously with warm water and leave to soak for 1 hour. Drain well, squeezing the excess water out. Finely chop the parsley and mint leaves—they should be chopped very small—and mix with the soaked and drained wheat. Add the diced cucumber. Stir well and then add most of the spring onions, keeping some back for the tomato salad.

Combine the lemon juice and olive oil and season well with salt and pepper to make a dressing. Pour most of it over the wheat mixture. Taste and adjust the seasoning as needed, then spoon onto a serving plate. Top with the cherry tomatoes, a scattering of the remaining spring onions, and the rest of the dressing.

When asparagus season comes around, the air can still be distinctly chilly—and chilly days call for warm, substantial salads. Here, the gently chewy barley grains mop up the wonderful flavors of the dressing.

Grilled asparagus and warm pearl barley salad with chive dressing

SERVES 4
PREPARATION TIME: 20 MINUTES
COOKING TIME: 50 MINUTES

2 tablespoons olive oil

1 leek, thinly sliced

1 heaping cup pearl barley

2 cups vegetable stock

one 14 oz can cannellini or other white beans, drained

12 medium asparagus spears, woody ends trimmed

FOR THE DRESSING:

juice of 2 lemons

1 egg yolk

¼ cup olive oil

a small bunch of chives, finely chopped, plus whole stalks, to serve (optional)

Heat a tablespoon of olive oil in a large saucepan and add the sliced leek. Cook gently for 5 minutes, stirring, until softened but not colored. Add the pearl barley, followed by the stock, and bring to a boil. Reduce the heat so that the liquid simmers gently and leave it to cook for about 40 minutes, or until nearly all the liquid is absorbed. The barley should be tender with a bit of bite. Stir in the drained beans and cook for a further 5 minutes to heat them through. Cover with a lid and set aside.

While the barley cooks, make the dressing. Whisk the lemon juice and egg yolk together in a bowl with a pinch of salt. As you continue whisking, gradually pour in the olive oil, drop by drop at first, to form a thick, creamy dressing. Stir in half the chopped chives and season to taste.

Place a griddle or grill pan over high heat. Coat the asparagus in the remaining tablespoon of olive oil and season well with salt and pepper. When the pan is smoking hot, spread the asparagus spears out in a single layer and grill them for 2–3 minutes, turning until partially blackened on all sides.

Serve the pearl barley in warmed bowls and top with the grilled asparagus, the dressing, the remaining chopped chives, and whole chive stalks (if using).

The contrasting toppings of this spiced, Indian-style salad sing with crisp pomegranate seeds and luscious yogurt. Texture is just as important as wonderful flavor and vibrant color in this dish.

Chana chaat

SERVES 4
PREPARATION TIME: 25 MINUTES
COOKING TIME: 25 MINUTES

FOR THE CHICKPEAS:

1 small onion, halved and sliced

¾ inch piece ginger, finely grated

1 green chili, deseeded and finely chopped

2 tablespoons peanut oil

1¾ cups cooked chickpeas, or one 14 oz can, drained

½ teaspoon mild chili powder

1 teaspoon garam masala

FOR THE REST:

½ cucumber, peeled, deseeded, and diced

2 vine tomatoes, diced

a squeeze of lemon

1 small bunch cilantro, roughly chopped, plus extra leaves, to serve

4 heaped tablespoons plain yogurt

seeds from 1 pomegranate

2 large cooked poppadoms, roughly crushed

Sauté the onion, ginger, and chili in the oil for 5 minutes until the onion is soft. Add the chickpeas and cook for a further 5 minutes until golden. Now add the chili powder and garam masala and cook for 2 minutes more. Remove from the heat, season well, and set aside to cool.

Mix the cucumber, tomatoes, lemon juice, and the chopped cilantro in a mixing bowl. Divide between 4 plates and top with the chickpea mixture, yogurt, pomegranate seeds, and the crushed poppadoms.

Sprinkle with the cilantro leaves and serve before the poppadoms soften.

Choose a really ripe Camembert or brie for this salad and the most luscious black figs you can lay your hands on, and you have the perfect partnership here. You could use the pickled fruit recipe on page 244 instead of the cooked figs if you prefer.

Camembert, watercress, and marinated figs with walnut dressing

SERVES 4
PREPARATION TIME: 25 MINUTES
PLUS MARINATING TIME
COOKING TIME: 10 MINUTES

¾ cup balsamic vinegar

scant ½ cup superfine sugar

2 garlic cloves, bruised

6 thyme sprigs

6 plump figs, halved

4 tablespoons walnut oil

a large handful of watercress, thick stalks trimmed

5½ oz ripe Camembert or brie, sliced

½ heaping cup walnuts, toasted and roughly chopped

Place the vinegar, sugar, garlic, and 4 of the thyme sprigs in a saucepan and add ⅓ cup plus 1 tablespoon of water. Bring to a boil and simmer for a minute to dissolve the sugar and cook out some of the vinegary flavor. Set aside to cool for 5 minutes, then pour over the halved figs and leave to marinate for an hour or two.

Discard the thyme sprigs and garlic from the marinade and spoon 5 tablespoons into a small lidded jar. Strip the leaves from the remaining 2 thyme sprigs and add to the jar with the walnut oil, a little salt, and plenty of pepper. Screw on the lid and shake well until combined to make a dressing.

Heat a nonstick frying pan over medium-high heat and sear the drained figs, cut sides down, for a minute or so until they caramelize. Remove the pan from the heat, turn the figs over, and set aside.

In a large bowl, drizzle the watercress with a little of the dressing, tossing to coat the leaves. Add the Camembert or brie, walnuts, and caramelized figs and divide between serving plates. Spoon the remaining dressing over each plate of salad.

Grilled lettuce: I know it sounds odd, but have faith. Lightly charred lettuce is an underrated beast and makes a very special Caesar salad. Be careful not to overcook the leaves, as they will lose their color and vibrancy—limp leaves are not what you want here.

Grilled Caesar salad

SERVES 4
PREPARATION TIME: 15 MINUTES
COOKING TIME: 10 MINUTES

1 garlic clove, crushed

scant ½ cup olive oil

6 Little Gem lettuces, halved lengthwise

1 egg yolk

1 teaspoon Dijon mustard

⅔ cup Parmesan

juice of ½ lemon

4 long, thin baguette slices

a handful of chopped flat-leaf parsley, to serve

Combine the garlic with the olive oil and brush a little over the lettuce halves. Season with salt and pepper.

Whisk the egg yolk in a bowl with the mustard and a tablespoon of finely grated Parmesan. As you continue whisking, very slowly pour in the remaining olive oil and garlic mixture until a thick dressing forms. Add the lemon juice and a tablespoon of water to thin the consistency a little.

Place a griddle or grill pan over high heat. Sear the lettuces, cut sides down first, until they begin to char—this will take about 2 minutes. Turn over and grill for a further 2 minutes or so. Finely grate enough Parmesan over the lettuce to lightly coat. Divide between serving plates.

Preheat the broiler and toast the baguette slices for a few minutes until golden on both sides. Spread a little dressing over one side and perch next to the lettuce. Drizzle the rest of the dressing over the salad and sprinkle with parsley and a few Parmesan shavings.

 Big Salads

Salad toppings

2

Toasted garlic bread crumbs

Warm about 3 tablespoons fruity olive oil in a large frying pan with 2 crushed garlic cloves and cook over a very low heat for a few minutes. Add a cupful of stale ciabatta or sourdough bread crumbs. Stir over medium heat for a few minutes until browned and toasted, then set aside to cool.

1

Maple walnuts

Coat ¾ cup walnuts with 2 tablespoons maple syrup, 1 tablespoon finely chopped rosemary, and a pinch of cayenne pepper. Season well. Spread on a baking tray lined with parchment paper. Cook at 325°F (Gas 2–3) for 15 minutes, stirring halfway, until golden. Cool before roughly chopping.

Tahini seeds

Spread 1¼ cups mixed seeds on a large baking tray and roast at 350°F (Gas 4) for 5 minutes. Combine 2 tablespoons light tahini paste, 1 tablespoon runny honey, ½ a crushed garlic clove, and 1 tablespoon sesame oil in a large bowl. Tip in the hot seeds and mix well. Spread out on the baking tray again and bake for another 5 minutes. Set aside to cool, then crumble over salads as needed.

3

4

Olive and polenta cubes

Stir 1⅓ cups quick-cooking polenta in 4 cups simmering veg stock for 3 minutes until thick. Add 1 large handful grated Parmesan and 4 tablespoons finely chopped black olives. Season well. Spread on a tray to a thickness of about 1 inch and cool. Once firm, cut the polenta into 1 inch cubes and sauté in olive oil until browned.

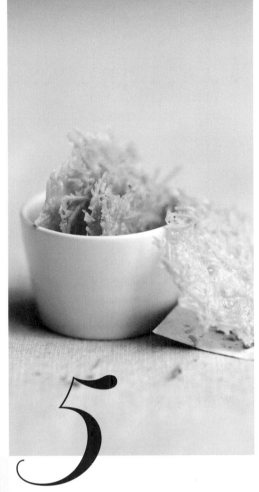

6

Roasted, spiced chickpeas

Thoroughly drain 5 cups chickpeas (freshly cooked or canned) then toss with 1 tablespoon olive oil, a pinch of cayenne, 1 teaspoon ground cumin, and 1 teaspoon ground coriander. Spread out on a baking tray lined with parchment paper. Cook for about 45 minutes at 350°F (Gas 4) until crisp and golden, shaking the tray every now and then to redistribute the chickpeas.

5

Crisp Parmesan lace

Line a large baking tray with parchment paper. Drop mounds of finely grated Parmesan on the tray at regular intervals (the cheese will spread out as it cooks) and bake at 400°F (Gas 6) for 3–4 minutes until golden and bubbling. Leave the cheese to settle for a minute, then remove with a spatula and leave to cool. Scatter over salads as they are, or break into pieces.

Soups

Chapter Four

This is for days when you can't bring yourself to have the oven on, because there's no cooking involved at all. The only potential hitch is that you'll need a juicer instead! It's a very satisfying dish, as the ripe avocado adds body and richness to all that raw vegetable virtue.

Raw vegetable and avocado soup

SERVES 4
PREPARATION TIME: 10 MINUTES

3 large carrots

1 cup spinach leaves

4 celery stalks

1¼ inch piece fresh ginger

2 large, very ripe avocados, halved and pitted

iced water

juice of ½ lime

1 tablespoon soy sauce

2–3 drops Tabasco sauce

ice cubes, toasted sesame oil, and cilantro leaves, to serve

Pass the carrots, spinach, celery, and ginger through a juicer and then transfer the juice to a blender. Blitz with the avocados until smooth. Make the quantity up to 3¼ cups with iced water, lime juice, soy, and Tabasco. Blend again.

Serve with ice cubes, a drop or 2 of sesame oil, and some perky cilantro leaves.

A vegetarian hot and sour soup is less complex than its fish- or meat-based counterparts, but what it loses in depth it gains in freshness and clarity. Vegetarian versions of fish sauce are readily available, but a little soy will do nicely instead. Serve this as a starter, part of a Southeast Asian meal, or a stand-alone soup.

Vietnamese hot and sour soup

SERVES 4–8
PREPARATION TIME: 20 MINUTES
COOKING TIME: 15 MINUTES

1 tablespoon peanut oil

2 shallots, finely sliced

2 lemongrass stalks, bruised with a rolling pin

2 garlic cloves, finely chopped

2 tablespoons sieved tamarind pulp or tamarind purée

2 tablespoons superfine sugar

3 cups vegetable stock (see page 236) or good-quality bought stock

2 celery stalks, sliced

2 tomatoes, cored and sliced into 8 pieces

¾ cup peeled and cored fresh pineapple, cut into cubes

1½ cups okra, thickly sliced

1½ cups bean sprouts

2 tablespoons vegetarian fish sauce or soy sauce

a small handful of cilantro, roughly chopped

a small handful of ngo om (rice paddy herb) or Thai basil leaves

Heat the oil in a large saucepan and add the shallots, lemongrass, garlic, tamarind pulp or purée, and sugar. Soften over a lowish heat for 5 minutes—you don't want the veg to color. Now add the vegetable stock and simmer for 5 minutes.

Throw in the celery, tomatoes, pineapple, and okra, and simmer for another few minutes. Add the bean sprouts and simmer for 5 minutes more. Shake in the vegetarian fish sauce or soy and taste the soup—you might want to add more tamarind, fish sauce, soy sauce, or sugar to balance the sweet and the sour.

Lastly, stir in the herbs and serve in small warmed bowls.

For some reason, lovage is a much underused culinary herb, and this chilled soup is a lovely way to discover its virtues. It is simplicity itself to make, as there's no real cooking involved. If lovage leaves are not forthcoming, celery leaves make a perfectly fine substitute.

Chilled cucumber and lovage soup

SERVES 4
PREPARATION TIME: 15 MINUTES

2 cucumbers, peeled and roughly sliced

6 oz crème fraîche

6 oz plain yogurt

1 tablespoon chopped lovage leaves

ice cubes and lovage leaves (optional), to serve

Place the cucumbers, ¾ cup of the crème fraîche, yogurt, and lovage leaves in a blender and liquidize until smooth. Season with salt and pepper to taste. Chill for a few hours.

Serve the chilled soup with teaspoonfuls of the remaining crème fraîche and ice cubes. If you wish, you could add a few lovage leaves to the bowls before serving.

Soups

This soup should taste of sunshine, so the ripest and freshest vegetables you can find will be needed to do it justice. If you want to gild the lily, some good black olives, pitted and diced, and a few oregano leaves are lovely when added to the vegetable garnish.

Gazpacho Andaluz

SERVES 4
PREPARATION TIME: 20 MINUTES
PLUS CHILLING TIME

1½ lb vine-ripened tomatoes

2 red peppers, halved and deseeded

1 large cucumber

1 garlic clove, crushed

½ loaf ciabatta, torn

4 tablespoons sherry vinegar

scant ½ cup extra virgin olive oil

2 teaspoons superfine sugar

Tabasco sauce, to serve (optional)

ice cubes and basil leaves, to serve

Set aside 2 tomatoes, half a red pepper, and a quarter of the cucumber.

Roughly chop the remaining tomatoes, peppers, and cucumber and place in a blender with the garlic and bread. Blend to a rough puree. Remove to a bowl, stir in the vinegar and ¾ cup plus 1 tablespoon of water, and season to taste with salt and pepper. Cover and chill for at least 2 hours or overnight. The bread will swell up and the flavors will mellow.

Before serving, nick the bases of the reserved tomatoes, place in a heatproof bowl, and cover with boiling water. Drain the tomatoes and peel the skin away. Chop into fine dice, along with the reserved red pepper and cucumber.

Stir the olive oil into the soup and taste again. Add the sugar, Tabasco sauce (if using) or a little more vinegar, salt or pepper, and even a little extra chilled water to adjust the consistency. The soup should have quite a kick to it, so make sure it's good and punchy.

Divide between cold bowls and serve with the ice cubes, a scattering of the diced vegetables, and basil leaves.

This list of ingredients rather bossily demands that you peel the green grapes. If the idea horrifies you or there simply aren't enough hours in your day, unpeeled grapes really won't be the end of the world. Whichever way you go, this unusual and subtle soup is wonderful.

White gazpacho

SERVES 4
PREPARATION TIME: 20 MINUTES
PLUS SOAKING AND CHILLING TIME

5-6 average slices, country-style bread (sourdough, for example)

1 cup milk

2 garlic cloves, finely chopped

½ cup blanched almonds

¾ cup extra virgin olive oil

2 tablespoons sherry vinegar

5½ oz green grapes, peeled, rinsed in lemon juice bath (to prevent browning), and halved

2 tablespoons blanched almonds, to serve

In a bowl, cover the bread with the milk and set aside for 20 minutes.

Place the soaked bread in a food processor with the garlic, blanched almonds, and a pinch of salt, then process until a purée forms.

Slowly add the olive oil in a steady stream while the motor is still running. Scrape into a bowl and stir in the vinegar with 2 cups cold water and salt and pepper to taste.

Cover and chill for at least 2 hours or overnight. Divide between chilled bowls and sprinkle with the grapes and blanched almonds.

Soups

The smoky depth of this soup comes from the magic chipotle pepper. You can buy it dried—in which case it will need soaking—or in jars. This will only get better if you have the chance to make it a day or two ahead.

Smoky black bean and roasted tomato soup

SERVES 4
PREPARATION TIME: 20 MINUTES
COOKING TIME: 55 MINUTES

FOR THE SALSA:

1 small red onion, very finely chopped

1 tablespoon sunflower oil

½ cup corn kernels

1 red chili, deseeded and finely chopped

a squeeze of lime

1 small bunch cilantro, leaves only

FOR THE SOUP:

1 tablespoon sunflower oil

2 red onions, chopped

3 garlic cloves, finely chopped

2 teaspoons chipotle pepper paste

1 teaspoon fresh or dried oregano

1 tablespoon cumin seeds

12 roasted tomato halves

4 cups cooked black beans

3 cups vegetable stock (see page 236) or good-quality bought stock

a squeeze of lime

sour cream, to serve

Start with the salsa. Cook the red onion in the sunflower oil for 5 minutes until soft and beginning to color. Turn up the heat and add the corn and chili, stirring until the corn is toasted at the edges. Remove from the heat, season with salt and pepper, and add a squeeze of lime.

To make the soup, heat the oil in a large saucepan, add the onions, and sauté slowly until translucent but not colored. Add the garlic, chipotle pepper or paste, oregano, and cumin seeds. Continue to cook for a further 5 minutes until the cumin is fragrant.

Add the roasted tomato halves, cooked beans, and vegetable stock, and bring to a boil. Simmer for 30 minutes. Season with salt, pepper, and lime juice, then liquidize in a blender until smooth. Check the seasoning and adjust if needed.

Stir the cilantro into the salsa.

Ladle the soup into warmed bowls and top with a spoonful of sour cream and a spoonful of salsa.

Soups

There might be a lot of chopping here, but this recipe is child's play and the result is special enough to warrant the extra effort. The cream adds a certain silky richness but can be left out without any ill effects. This is lovely served cool the next day—the vegetables may not be as sprightly but will have gained wisdom and character.

Summer minestrone

SERVES 4
PREPARATION TIME: 15 MINUTES
COOKING TIME: 45 MINUTES

2 tablespoons olive oil

2 garlic cloves, finely chopped

2 shallots, finely chopped

2 celery stalks, finely chopped

1 fennel bulb, finely chopped

1 heaping cup young fava beans, pods and skins removed

1⅓ cups young fresh peas, shelled weight

1½ cups green beans, sliced

2 cups asparagus tips, sliced

4 cups vegetable stock (see page 236) or good-quality bought stock

a handful each of mint and basil leaves

¼ cup heavy cream

4 tablespoons fresh pesto (see page 238), to serve

Heat the olive oil in a large saucepan and soften the garlic, shallots, celery, and fennel. It should take about 10 minutes.

Add half the fava beans, peas, green beans, and asparagus. Cook, stirring, for 5 minutes. Pour in the stock, bring to a boil, and simmer for about 25 minutes.

Add the other half of the vegetables to the saucepan and cook for 5 minutes more. Remove from the heat and pour in a little extra boiling water if the soup appears too thick for your liking. Add the herbs and cream and season to taste.

Ladle into warmed bowls and drop a spoonful of pesto into each to serve.

The humble potato has been ruthlessly fired from chowder duty and replaced with the more vivacious butternut squash, cubes of which dot this pale soup like orange jewels. But either vegetable works well in this dish, so don't hesitate to reinstate potato if you have some on hand—1 lb 2 oz will do nicely—to produce a slightly milder soup.

Winter squash and corn chowder

SERVES 4
PREPARATION TIME: 20 MINUTES
COOKING TIME: 25 MINUTES

1 small butternut squash

3 tablespoons butter

1 small onion, finely chopped

1 fennel bulb, finely chopped

1 carrot, finely chopped

1 garlic clove, finely chopped

½ teaspoon dried chili flakes

2 tablespoons all-purpose flour

3 cups vegetable stock (see page 236) or good-quality bought stock

1 cup whole milk

2 corn cobs, kernels sliced off

a small bunch of dill, finely chopped

a squeeze of lime, to taste

Peel the butternut squash with a swivel vegetable peeler. Cut in half lengthwise, scoop out the seeds, and dice the flesh into large cubes.

Melt the butter in a large, deep saucepan. Add the onion, fennel, carrot, and garlic, and cook gently for 10 minutes, stirring often, until softened but not colored. Add the chili flakes and flour and stir for a further minute, followed by the cubed squash and vegetable stock. Bring to a boil and simmer for 10 minutes or so until the squash is tender.

Add the milk, corn kernels, and dill and simmer for 5 minutes more. Season well and add a squeeze of lime.

Soups

Sometimes a rich main course demands a very light starter to get the ball rolling, and this fits the bill very prettily: a clear, ruby broth that will tempt but not overstuff your eager diners. Do try to avoid beets that are ready-cooked, vinegared, and wrapped in plastic—what you want is the fresh stuff full of all that sweet, earthy flavor.

Beet and porcini broth

SERVES 4
PREPARATION TIME: 10 MINUTES
COOKING TIME: 30 MINUTES
PLUS STEEPING TIME

¾ oz dried porcini

3 large beets, peeled and roughly chopped

2 carrots, roughly chopped

1 celery stalk, roughly chopped

a handful of chervil including stalks, plus extra sprigs to garnish

TO SEASON:

a squeeze of lemon

1 teaspoon superfine sugar

Place all the ingredients in a large saucepan with 28 fl oz water. Bring to a boil very slowly and simmer gently for 30 minutes. Remove from the heat and leave to stand for 20 minutes, then strain through a fine sieve. Reserve the mushrooms and one of the beets.

Finely dice the porcini and the reserved beet and add to the strained broth. Season with the lemon juice, sugar, and some salt and pepper.

Divide between bowls and garnish with chervil sprigs.

Celery root soup is heavenly and loves being made in advance—perhaps the night before you plan to eat it—to give the ingredients time to get to know each other. The soup will then be ready to be reheated and served hot, or it works extremely well eaten chilled.

Butter bean and celery root velouté with charmoula

SERVES 4
PREPARATION TIME: 20 MINUTES
COOKING TIME: 35 MINUTES

1 celery root, about 1 lb, cubed

a squeeze of lemon

2 celery stalks, finely chopped

1 onion, finely chopped

2 garlic cloves, chopped

2 tablespoons olive oil

1¾ cups cooked butter beans

½ teaspoon salt

2 tablespoons crème fraîche (optional)

4 tablespoons charmoula dressing
(see page 244)

Drop the cubed celery root into a bowl of cold water with a squeeze of lemon. This will stop it browning.

Cook the chopped celery, onion, and garlic in the olive oil for 10 minutes until soft and translucent but not brown. Add the celery root and cook for a further 5 minutes, then tip the butter beans in with 3¼ cups water and the salt. Bring to a boil and simmer for about 20 minutes.

Liquidize in a blender with the crème fraîche (if using) until completely smooth. For a truly velvety soup, push the mixture through a sieve. Adjust the seasoning. Serve chilled or reheat gently until piping hot. Add a spoonful of charmoula dressing to each serving.

Breads

Chapter Five

You can use all plain white flour in this recipe to make it a bit more refined, or half rye or spelt flour to increase the nutty overtones. The dough might look sticky and shaggy when all the ingredients are mixed together, but don't worry—it's meant to look that way. And remember that a light hand really does produce a light soda bread.

Quick soda bread

MAKES 1 LARGE LOAF
PREPARATION TIME: 15 MINUTES
COOKING TIME: 45 MINUTES

1⅔ cups all-purpose flour

1⅔ cups whole wheat flour

1 tablespoon superfine sugar

1 teaspoon baking soda

1 teaspoon salt

2 tablespoons chilled butter, cubed

2⅔ cups buttermilk

Preheat the oven to 400°F (Gas 6) and line a baking tray with parchment paper.

Sift the flours into a mixing bowl and add back in all the bran you catch in the sieve except for 1 tablespoon, which you need to reserve for later. Stir in the sugar, baking soda, and salt. Rub in the butter with your fingertips.

Quickly stir in the buttermilk and mix with a palette knife to form a rough dough. Don't overwork the mixture or it will be tough, and work quickly as you form the dough into a round loaf. Sit the dough on the lined baking tray and make a deep cross in the top with a sharp knife. Sprinkle with the reserved tablespoon of bran and bake for about 45 minutes until golden and hollow-sounding when tapped underneath.

Cool on a wire rack, covering with a clean dishtowel if you prefer the crust to soften slightly.

Breads

This pizza-style rolled-up bread is a deliciously easy solution when famished crowds descend. Stromboli freeze incredibly well, so pop one loaf in the freezer and defrost when needed: just heat through in a warm oven and it will be nearly as good as the day it was made.

Olive stromboli

MAKES 2 LARGE LOAVES
PREPARATION TIME: 30 MINUTES
PLUS RESTING TIME
COOKING TIME: 30 MINUTES

1 teaspoon superfine sugar

1 tablespoon rapid-rise dry yeast

3 cups lukewarm water

5⅓ cups bread flour, plus extra for dusting

1 tablespoon salt

2 tablespoons cornmeal or polenta, for dusting

extra virgin olive oil, for oiling and drizzling

FOR THE FILLING:

a large handful of basil leaves

20 black olives, pitted

¾ cup roasted red peppers in olive oil, drained

1 ball buffalo mozzarella, torn into pieces

In a large bowl, mix the sugar, yeast, and lukewarm water and set aside for 10 minutes to "proof," or begin the fermentation process. Add half the flour and mix well with a spoon. Set aside in a warm place for another 15 minutes.

Now add the salt and remaining flour and mix to form a rough dough—use a wooden spoon at first, and when the dough becomes difficult to stir, use your hands instead. Turn onto a lightly floured surface and knead for at least 10 minutes (or 5 minutes in a machine with a dough hook) until smooth and elastic. The dough will be very sticky at first, but don't be tempted to add extra flour; its stickiness makes the finished loaf light. Turn the dough into an oiled bowl, cover with a damp, clean dishtowel and leave in a warm place for an hour or until doubled in size.

Preheat the oven to 400°F (Gas 6) and dust a large, oiled baking tray with a little cornmeal or polenta.

When ready, knock the dough back with a punch. Divide in half and roll or stretch each piece out on a floured surface to form a large rectangle about 8 x 12 inches. Scatter half the basil leaves, olives, peppers, and mozzarella over the surface and drizzle with a little olive oil. You now need to roll up the stromboli. With the dough placed long side toward you, gently roll each piece of dough and its filling into a long log shape.

Cover the stromboli with a damp, clean dishtowel and set aside for 15 minutes. Drizzle with olive oil, scatter with a little sea salt, and bake for 30 minutes or so until golden and risen. Cool on a wire rack for at least 10 minutes before slicing.

Let no one tell you that making your own bread requires some kind of talent or special culinary gift. With a little patience (the resting time is long, but it gives this bread its lovely flavor) a chewy and characterful sourdough will be yours with barely a knead.

No-knead sourdough loaf

MAKES 1 LOAF
PREPARATION TIME: 15 MINUTES
PLUS RESTING TIME
COOKING TIME: ABOUT 45 MINUTES

1⅔ cups strong whole wheat bread flour (or bread flour), plus extra for dusting

1⅔ cups white bread flour

¼ teaspoon rapid-rise yeast

1½ teaspoons salt

1½ cups warm water

sunflower oil, for oiling

Combine all the dry ingredients in a large bowl and add the water, stirring with a wooden spoon and then with your hands, to form very soft, sticky dough. It will look shaggy but you don't need to overmix it. Cover the bowl with plastic wrap and leave in a warm place for 15–18 hours.

Lightly flour a work surface and flour your hands—just a little is needed. Fold the dough over on itself, cover with oiled plastic wrap, and leave for 15 minutes.

Again using minimal flour on your hands and work surface, shape the dough into a ball and slide it onto a sheet of parchment paper sprinkled with whole wheat flour. Cover with a clean dishtowel and leave for 2 hours until doubled in size.

Before the dough has finished rising, place a large, lidded casserole in the oven and preheat to 425°F (Gas 7). When the oven is ready, carefully take the hot casserole out, place the dough inside, and replace the lid. Return to the oven for 30 minutes, then remove the lid and cook for a further 15 minutes or so until the bread is golden on top. Tip out of the casserole and cool on a wire rack.

Breads

Think of this as an extraordinary flatbread rather than your usual pizza. It's rolled out slightly thicker than conventional pizza dough and comes out soft and airy in the middle. Don't be fooled by the simple ingredients: it's a heavenly combination and, served straight from the oven, goes beautifully with soups, salads, dips, or roasted vegetables.

Pizza bianca

MAKES 4
PREPARATION TIME: 15 MINUTES
PLUS RESTING TIME
COOKING TIME: 5–10 MINUTES PER PIZZA

1⅔ cups all-purpose flour

1⅔ cups white bread flour

1 teaspoon rapid-rise dry yeast

2 teaspoons salt

1½ cups warm water

4 tablespoons extra virgin olive oil

cornmeal or polenta, for dusting

rosemary leaves and sea salt, to scatter over

Combine the flours, yeast, salt, and warm water in an electric mixer or mixing bowl to form dough. Add a tablespoon of the olive oil. Use a dough hook to knead for 5–8 minutes, or turn onto a lightly floured surface and knead by hand for 10 minutes until the dough is smooth and elastic. Place in an oiled bowl, cover with plastic wrap, and leave to rest in a warm place for an hour.

Preheat the oven to 450°F (Gas 8) and, if you own a pizza stone or heatproof tile that will fit inside the oven, now is the time to put it in to heat.

Knock back the dough with a punch. Roll out a quarter of the dough on a floured surface (don't use lots of flour) until it forms a circle about ½ inch thick. Dust a baking tray with cornmeal or polenta and lay the pizza on it. Drizzle with olive oil and scatter with rosemary and sea salt. Carefully put the tray in the oven—onto the hot pizza stone or tile (if using)—and cook for a few minutes. The timing will very much depend on your oven, but it shouldn't be more than 8–10 minutes. While this one's cooking, prepare the next pizza, and bake each one in quick succession. Serve each cooked pizza hot and straight out of the oven.

Like the soda bread recipe on page 130, this recipe is quick, so you won't find any yeast here. It's an ideal mixture to experiment with: you can bake it as a whole loaf or vary the herbs and the root vegetables as you wish. This bread is forgiving and versatile but always best served warm, preferably with a bowl of hot soup.

Parsnip and rosemary rolls

MAKES 6
PREPARATION TIME: 15 MINUTES
COOKING TIME: 25 MINUTES

olive oil, to oil and drizzle

1½ cups coarsely grated parsnips

1¾ cups self-rising flour

1 tablespoon chopped rosemary, plus extra sprigs

1 teaspoon salt

2 eggs, beaten

2 tablespoons milk

Preheat the oven to 375°F (Gas 5). Oil a baking tray or line it with parchment paper.

Mix the parsnips, flour, rosemary, and salt in a large bowl. Make a well in the center and add the beaten eggs and milk. Use a knife to quickly mix everything together to form a rough dough, being careful not to overwork it. Divide the dough into six pieces and shape each into a round. Slash the tops with a sharp knife and press a small rosemary sprig onto each. Drizzle with olive oil.

Bake for about 25–30 minutes until golden. Cool on a wire rack if you like, but these rolls are best eaten warm.

Fast Feasts

Chapter Six

This makes a complete supper; it's well balanced and quick, quick, quick. Tempeh is tofu's often overlooked cousin made from fermented soybeans. Alternatively, you could use firm tofu here. The Indian cottage cheese, paneer, would work too.

Tamarind tempeh with sesame noodles and shredded greens

SERVES 2
PREPARATION TIME: 15 MINUTES
PLUS MARINATING TIME
COOKING TIME: 10 MINUTES

1⅓ cups tempeh, sliced ¾ inch thick

1½ inch piece ginger, finely chopped

finely grated zest and juice of
1 small orange

2 tablespoons mild honey

2 tablespoons tamarind paste or purée

2 tablespoons soy sauce,
plus extra to serve

2 cups medium egg noodles

a little toasted sesame oil

2 tablespoons peanut oil

1 green chili, deseeded and
finely chopped

1 garlic clove, finely chopped

3 cups shredded Asian greens

2 teaspoons gomashio (see page 236)

2 spring onions, finely shredded

Coat the sliced tempeh with a mixture of half the chopped ginger, the orange zest, honey, tamarind, and 1 tablespoon soy sauce. Ideally, leave to marinate for 10–30 minutes.

Cook the noodles according to package instructions, refresh under cold water, and drain. Toss with a very little sesame oil to prevent sticking, and set aside. Heat 1 tablespoon peanut oil in a large wok or frying pan, and when it is almost smoking add the tempeh and stir-fry for a few minutes, or until browned on all sides. Remove to a plate.

Pour the remaining peanut oil into the pan and add the rest of the ginger, chili, and garlic. Cook and stir for a minute, then add the greens. Return the tempeh to the wok or pan and add the orange juice, then toss over the heat until the greens wilt.

Now add the drained noodles and toss. Divide between two warmed bowls and dot with a few drops of sesame oil. Sprinkle with gomashio and finish with the spring onion shreds. Offer more soy sauce at the table.

Fast Feasts

This raw carpaccio is so pretty and can be ready in a jiffy. Some soft cheese spooned or crumbled over the sliced vegetables will make it a little more sustaining. However, you might prefer to let the dressing sing through on its own for a wonderfully light lunch or supper.

Summer vegetable carpaccio with horseradish dressing

SERVES 2
PREPARATION TIME: 15 MINUTES

2 ripe but firm baby avocados, halved and pitted

juice of ½ lemon

2 radishes, with leaves, scrubbed

3 baby carrots

2 baby zucchini

2½ inch piece cucumber, peeled, halved, and deseeded

1 tablespoon extra virgin olive oil

3 tablespoons horseradish dressing (see page 238)

1 tablespoon alfalfa sprouts or pea shoots

Peel the avocados, scoring the skin lengthwise first. Use a very sharp knife to shave the flesh into long slices, and toss with a little of the lemon juice to prevent browning.

Slice the radishes (set aside the leaves), carrots, and zucchini lengthwise and pare the cucumber into ribbons with a vegetable peeler. Toss with the radish leaves and the remaining lemon juice and add to the avocados along with the olive oil. Season to taste and arrange on two plates. Spoon the horseradish dressing over and scatter with the sprouts or pea shoots.

This is a pretty but complex little number: by turns salty, crisp, hot, sour, yielding, and sweet. It will serve three as a swift starter or two as a summery supper. Make the preparation even quicker by mixing the dressing in advance, so you have it ready in the refrigerator.

Carrot fritters with halloumi and sweet lemon dressing

SERVES 2–3
PREPARATION TIME: 15 MINUTES
PLUS CHILLING TIME
COOKING TIME: ABOUT 10 MINUTES

FOR THE FRITTERS:

9 oz halloumi

4 large carrots, coarsely grated or shredded

5 spring onions, finely sliced

a small bunch of cilantro, leaves chopped

1 tablespoon coriander seeds, toasted and crushed

2 tablespoons gram or chickpea flour (or all-purpose flour)

2 eggs, beaten

TO FINISH:

3 tablespoons olive oil

a handful of arugula leaves

4 tablespoons sweet lemon dressing (see page 238)

Coarsely grate a quarter of the halloumi and add to the carrots in a mixing bowl. Slice the remaining halloumi and set aside. Add the remaining fritter ingredients to the mixing bowl, season with pepper and just a little salt, and mix well. Form into 12 round cakes, flattening them with your hand, and lay out on a tray. If you have time, chill for 30 minutes to firm them up.

Heat the olive oil in a pan and fry the cakes for a couple of minutes on each side until golden. Remove to a plate and keep warm in a low oven while you fry the halloumi for a minute or two on each side. You won't need any extra oil for this. When done, the cakes should be crisp and golden.

Layer the fritters and halloumi slices on serving plates with the arugula, and drizzle with the sweet lemon dressing.

Fast Feasts

This eggplant is happy to be a light and summery supper option when you'd rather not spend much time in the kitchen. Make sure the eggplant is cooked to buttery tenderness before covering with the miso mixture, and it will be sublime. If you love the taste of sesame, include a few drops of sesame oil in the miso topping.

Japanese eggplant with miso

SERVES 4
PREPARATION TIME: 15 MINUTES
COOKING TIME: 6–8 MINUTES

2 tablespoons white miso paste

2 tablespoons superfine sugar

1 tablespoon mirin

1 tablespoon rice wine vinegar

4 Japanese eggplants or baby eggplants

2 tablespoons peanut oil

2 spring onions, finely shredded

2 tablespoons sprouts, ideally shiso, or wild coriander

2 teaspoons sesame seeds, lightly toasted

steamed rice and pickled (sushi) ginger, to serve

Combine the miso, sugar, mirin and rice wine vinegar, stirring until smooth. Cut the eggplant into 1¼ inch thick slices and brush with peanut oil on both sides. Preheat the broiler and arrange the eggplant slices on a baking sheet in a single layer. Cook, positioned away from the heating element, for 2 minutes on one side, then turn the slices over and broil for another couple of minutes until golden and cooked through.

Smear a little topping over each of the eggplant slices and pop them under the broiler for a further 2 minutes or so. You want the topping to be caramelized and bubbling.

Scatter the grilled eggplant with shredded spring onions, sprouts, and sesame seeds and serve with some steamed rice and pickled ginger.

If you've fallen into the habit of boiling or steaming cauliflower, try this idea. It takes mere minutes of pan-frying, and the humble brassica's best nutty, sweet notes are magically unlocked. It may seem simple, but its depth of flavor justifies its place as a stand-alone meal.

Charred baby cauliflower with cumin, chili, and almonds

SERVES 4
PREPARATION TIME: 10 MINUTES
COOKING TIME: 10 MINUTES

3 tablespoons olive oil

4 baby cauliflowers, separated into small florets

1½ teaspoons cumin seeds

2 garlic cloves, finely sliced

1 red chili, deseeded and finely sliced

¾ cup sliced almonds

1 tablespoon extra virgin olive oil

2 tablespoons chopped flat-leaf parsley

Using a large wok or a deep frying pan, heat the olive oil and add the cauliflower, frying until darkly golden at the edges. Reduce the heat, cover with a lid or a baking sheet, and cook for 1–2 minutes.

Add the cumin seeds, garlic, chili, and almonds. Stir-fry for 5 minutes over medium heat until the almonds are golden. Season generously with salt and pepper, drizzle with the extra virgin olive oil, and scatter with parsley.

This is an easy recipe that hardly needs to meet the heat, and ideal for an Indian summer when celery root is just coming into season. The yogurt in the dressing makes this lighter than traditional rémoulades; if you need more sustenance, serve it with some grilled bread.

Celery root rémoulade with capers and grain mustard

SERVES 4
PREPARATION TIME: 20 MINUTES

1 medium celery root, about 1¼ lb

juice of 1 lemon

1 egg yolk

1 teaspoon whole-grain mustard

scant ½ cup mild olive oil

2 heaped tablespoons plain yogurt

2 teaspoons finely chopped flat-leaf parsley, plus extra to serve

2 teaspoons finely chopped chives

2 tablespoons baby capers, plus a few extra to serve

a few red endive or radicchio leaves, to serve

Cut the celery root into quarters and use a vegetable peeler to pare it into wide ribbons. Stack a few ribbons on top of each other to form small piles and slice into fine matchsticks. Fill a mixing bowl with water and lemon juice, and add the shredded celery root as you go to prevent it from turning brown.

Use a mini food processor or a bowl and a whisk to make the dressing: Start by blending the egg yolk with a large pinch of sea salt, the mustard, and 2 tablespoons of the lemon juice. Begin adding the olive oil, drop by drop at first, as you blend or whisk, slowly graduating to a thin, steady stream. When the mixture is thick and all the oil has been added, stir in the yogurt and chopped herbs. Add the rinsed, drained, and roughly chopped capers, along with some freshly ground black pepper. Taste and season with extra lemon juice or perhaps a little salt if needed.

Blanch the celery root in plenty of boiling water for 30 seconds then tip into a colander and refresh under cold running water. Drain thoroughly and pat dry with a clean dishtowel. Toss with the dressing in a large mixing bowl, divide between serving plates with the red endive leaves, and scatter with extra parsley and capers.

Perfectly cooked tofu will absorb very little oil, so it emerges from the pan golden, crisp, and light. The trick is to press the tofu and dry it very thoroughly before cooking it briefly. Keep your oil hot, and place the cooked tofu on absorbent paper towels when it's done.

Crispy five-spice tofu with soy dipping sauce

SERVES 4
PREPARATION TIME: 20 MINUTES
COOKING TIME: 10 MINUTES

FOR THE TOFU:

2⅔ cups cubed firm tofu

6 tablespoons cornstarch

2 tablespoons five-spice powder

1 teaspoon dried chili flakes

5 tablespoons peanut oil

FOR THE SOY DIPPING SAUCE:

4 tablespoons soy sauce

2 tablespoons rice wine vinegar

1 teaspoon toasted sesame oil

¾ inch piece ginger, very finely chopped

1 teaspoon superfine sugar

Place the tofu on a plate lined with a double layer of paper towels. Cover the tofu with another double layer of paper towels, followed by a plate, and press down firmly. Weigh the plate down with a couple of unopened cans and set aside while you prepare the rest of the recipe. Turn the oven on to a very low setting—you only need to keep the cooked tofu warm.

To make the soy dipping sauce, combine all the ingredients in a bowl, stirring to dissolve the sugar.

Now continue with the tofu. Combine the cornstarch, five-spice, and chili flakes on a plate and spread out evenly. Measure half the oil into a large, stable wok and set over a low–medium flame to heat slowly. Pat the tofu dry with more paper towels. Roll the cubes in the cornstarch mixture until well coated on all sides. Turn up the heat under the wok and fry half the tofu cubes, turning carefully with tongs, until crisp and golden on all sides. This will take about 5 minutes. Transfer to a plate lined with paper towels to soak up any excess oil, and place in the oven to keep warm. Repeat with the remaining oil and tofu, then serve straightaway with the dipping sauce alongside.

Fast Feasts

Protein-rich tofu has a mild and delicate flavor, making it the ideal carrier for other tastes like sesame, soy, chili, ginger, and garlic. Depending on how firm your tofu is, you can slice it and add to things like salads and stir-fries.

How to make tofu

nigari + H₂O

160°F–175°F

step 2.

Dissolve 2 teaspoons of powdered nigari in ½ cup lukewarm water and gradually add to the soy milk, stirring constantly. If you can't find nigari, use 2 cups white wine vinegar or lemon juice and no water. The soy milk will begin to separate and curdle and look like curds and whey.

step 1.

Pour 2 cups unsweetened soy milk into a pan and boil for about 5 minutes. Stand a liquid thermometer in the pan and allow the milk to cool to 160–175°F.

tofu curds

step 3.

Remove from the heat and leave alone for 15 minutes. Large curds should have formed, but if they look small, stir in another teaspoon of dissolved nigari. Ladle out some of the liquid tofu whey and discard. Line a colander with several layers of damp cheesecloth and stand in a large bowl to catch any liquid. Carefully ladle the solid tofu curds into the colander.

soy beans

Soy milk, made from soy beans, forms the basis of making tofu. Nigari (magnesium chloride) is a tofu coagulator that causes the soy milk to separate into curds and whey, rather like the process in cheese making. Powdered nigari can be found in Japanese food shops, but you can use white wine vinegar or lemon juice instead, adding extra as needed until the soy milk curdles.

tofu

water

20 minutes

press

cold water

step 5.

Carefully unmold the drained tofu into a bowl of cold water to remove any bitterness. Soak for 10 minutes, then refresh with new water and leave to soak for a further 10 minutes.

step 4.

Sit a small plate on top, weigh it down with unopened cans, and leave for 20 minutes to firm up.

step 6.

Use straightaway or gently transfer the tofu to a lidded container, cover with cold water, and chill for up to 3 days.

The little ear shapes of orecchiette collect robust sauces better than any other pasta shape, but any small shell-like variety will work well. Don't be scared of cooking the broccoli until truly soft—it doesn't take long and this is not the time for fancy, al dente vegetables.

Orecchiette pasta with broccoli and pine nuts

SERVES 4
PREPARATION TIME: 15 MINUTES
COOKING TIME: 15 MINUTES

½ lb purple sprouting or tenderstem broccoli, roughly chopped

12 oz dried orecchiette pasta

4 tablespoons extra virgin olive oil

1 chili, deseeded and finely chopped

2 fat garlic cloves, finely sliced

½ cup pine nuts, toasted until golden

2 tablespoons finely grated pecorino

Blanch the broccoli in plenty of boiling water for 3 minutes or so. Drain in a colander and refresh under cold running water. Drain again and roughly chop.

Cook the orecchiette in plenty of salted boiling water for 9–11 minutes until al dente, or according to package instructions. While the pasta cooks, combine the olive oil, chili, and garlic in a cold frying pan, place over medium heat, and cook until the garlic is fragrant but not browned. Add the chopped broccoli, cover with a lid or baking sheet, and cook very gently for a few minutes. Season well with salt and pepper and stir in the pine nuts.

Drain the pasta, reserving a couple of tablespoons of the cooking water. Tip into the frying pan with the broccoli mixture and add the pecorino and reserved cooking water. Mix well and serve.

These crisp and tender potato cakes are divine served with softly poached eggs and a punchy salsa verde. The trick to neat poached eggs is to use the freshest you can find. If you form the potato cakes a few hours ahead of time, cooking them will be a breeze.

Salad potato griddle cakes with olives and poached eggs

SERVES 4
PREPARATION TIME: 10 MINUTES
PLUS COOLING TIME
COOKING TIME: 25 MINUTES

1 lb 2 oz small salad potatoes, such as Red Bliss or Yellow Finn

2 shallots, very finely chopped

2 tablespoons black olives, pitted and roughly chopped

1 tablespoon chopped flat-leaf parsley

1¾ oz pecorino sardo, shaved

5 very fresh eggs

1 heaped tablespoon potato flour or plain flour, plus extra to dust

3–4 tablespoons olive oil

4 tablespoons salsa verde dressing (see page 238)

Scrub the potatoes and boil in their skins in salted water for 15 minutes, or until just tender. Drain, allow to cool for 15 minutes, and then crush roughly with a fork. Add the shallots, olives, parsley, and half the cheese. Season generously with freshly ground black pepper and just a little salt, and taste the mixture to make sure the seasoning is balanced. Beat 1 egg and mix into the potatoes along with the flour. Form the mixture into 8 flat cakes, using floured hands.

Space the cakes out on a plate and chill for at least 1 hour or overnight. Before cooking, generously brush the potato cakes with olive oil on both sides. Heat a large griddle or grill pan and slowly brown the cakes for about 4 minutes on each side, in batches if necessary. Keep warm while you cook the remaining eggs.

Heat a deep frying pan of water until it just reaches boiling point, then reduce the heat so the base is covered in tiny bubbles. Carefully crack in the eggs, one by one, as gently as you can. Poach the eggs for 3 minutes until the whites are just set, then remove from the pan with a slotted spoon and drain on paper towels.

Serve a poached egg on each pair of cakes, with the salsa verde spooned over and the remaining pecorino shavings.

Fast Feasts

Even though fried rice is pretty quick to make, you need to start the day before, as cooked, chilled rice is essential to get the authentic fried rice texture. Use rice left over from another dish if you have some, but ensure it's no more than one day old, and was chilled within an hour of cooking. Once the rice is done, the rest is easy.

Cashew fried rice

SERVES 4
PREPARATION TIME: 10 MINUTES
PLUS CHILLING TIME
COOKING TIME: 25 MINUTES

2⅔ cups cold, cooked Thai fragrant or basmati rice (or 1¼ cups uncooked rice)

14 oz mixed vegetables, such as sugar snap peas, snow peas, baby corn, peas

2 tablespoons peanut oil

⅔ cup shelled cashews

2 garlic cloves, finely chopped

1½ inch piece ginger, finely chopped

2 eggs, beaten

1 teaspoon toasted sesame oil

1–2 tablespoons soy sauce

chili tomato jam (see page 242), to serve

If using the uncooked rice, start the day before. Rinse the rice well in a sieve held under cold running water and place the drained rice in a saucepan. Add enough cold water to cover the rice by about ¾ inch. Bring to a boil and simmer for 10 minutes until the water is absorbed. Cover the pan, remove from the heat, and set aside to steam for 10 minutes. Fluff the rice up with a fork, and as soon as it's cool, cover with plastic wrap and chill overnight.

When you're ready to fry the rice, blanch the vegetables in boiling water for 2 minutes. Drain in a colander and refresh under cold running water.

Heat the oil in a wok, throw in the cashews, and stir-fry until golden. Remove to a bowl with a slotted spoon. Add the garlic and ginger to the wok and cook for a minute, then add the cold rice and vegetables, and stir-fry for a good 2 minutes to heat through. Push everything to the side of the pan and tip in the egg and sesame oil, stirring occasionally to form a sort of omelette. Break the omelette into pieces with the spatula and mix into the rice, then add the cashews. Season with the soy sauce and serve with the chili tomato jam on the side.

It's official: sticks of celery root trump toast fingers for dunking into softly boiled duck eggs and turn breakfast fare into a stylish supper. Hands-on cooking time is minimal, so while the "chips" crisp themselves in the oven, you have a chance to relax and unwind after work.

Soft-boiled duck egg with celery root dipping chips

SERVES 2
PREPARATION TIME: 15 MINUTES
COOKING TIME: 35 MINUTES

1 large celery root, about 1¾ lb thickly sliced

2 tablespoons mild olive oil

1 teaspoon celery salt, plus extra for the eggs

a pinch of cayenne pepper

2 duck eggs

Preheat the oven to 450°F (Gas 8). Cut the celery root slices into fat chips and plunge into a pan of salted, boiling water for 2 minutes. Drain in a colander, then coat with the olive oil, celery salt, and cayenne pepper. Spread out in a single layer on a large baking sheet and bake for about 30 minutes.

When the chips are 25 minutes into their cooking time, lower the duck eggs into a saucepan of boiling water and simmer gently for 6 minutes. Remove from the water and gingerly (they'll be hot!) slice the tops off. Sit each egg in an egg cup ready for dipping. Sprinkle with a little more celery salt and accompany with golden celery chips fresh from the oven.

Fast Feasts

Rigatoni is a ridged, tube-shaped pasta that goes perfectly with this comforting walnut sauce. It's not chili hot, merely warm and toasty, making it the perfect fast food for a crisp autumn night. Serve the pasta with a tangle of buttery spinach on the side if you wish.

Chili and crushed walnut rigatoni

SERVES 4
PREPARATION TIME: 15 MINUTES
COOKING TIME: 15 MINUTES

2½ cups walnut halves

1 tablespoon extra virgin olive oil

1 red chili, deseeded and finely chopped

½ garlic clove, crushed

1 teaspoon thyme leaves

2 heaped tablespoons mascarpone

2 tablespoons finely grated Parmesan

12 oz dried rigatoni pasta or similar short pasta shapes

Toast the walnuts in a dry frying pan, tossing often until golden and fragrant. Tip onto a chopping board and, when cool enough, roughly chop. Some nuts should be very fine, some larger.

Place the olive oil, chili, and garlic in a cold frying pan and heat gently—you don't want the garlic to color. After a minute or two remove the pan from the heat and stir in the thyme, followed by the mascarpone and Parmesan. Season with salt and pepper. Stir in nearly all the walnuts—keeping a couple of tablespoons back—and set aside.

Cook the pasta until al dente in a pot of salted, boiling water according to package instructions. Drain in a colander, reserving a few tablespoons of cooking water, and immediately return the pasta to the saucepan with the reserved water. Add the walnut sauce and toss through. Serve with the reserved walnuts sprinkled over.

Tomatoes

2

Panzanella burrata

Roughly dice 3 ripe vine tomatoes and mix with 5-6 average slices sourdough bread, torn into chunks and toasted in the oven. Dress with extra virgin olive oil, red wine vinegar, salt, pepper, and fresh basil. Rest at room temperature for 1–2 hours. Mix in half a small, finely chopped onion and serve spooned over a globe of fresh burrata or buffalo mozzarella.

1

Simple salad

Halve or slice a plateful of tomato varieties, depending on their size, and spread out on a serving plate. Whisk 3 tablespoons light cream into 3 tablespoons olive oil with 2 tablespoons white wine vinegar, a pinch each of superfine sugar and salt, and plenty of cracked black pepper. Drizzle over the tomatoes and scatter with fresh mint.

Shopska salad

Core and dice 4 large tomatoes, chop 2 deseeded red peppers, and cube a 6 inch peeled and deseeded cucumber. Slice ½ small red onion very finely, and finely chop 2 tablespoons parsley leaves. Combine the tomatoes, peppers, cucumber, red onion, and parsley and dress with red wine vinegar, mild olive oil, salt, and pepper. Coarsely grate 3½ oz feta over the top before serving.

3

4

Tomato and tarragon tart

Preheat the oven to 350°F (Gas 4). Line a 4½ x 14 inch pan with shortcrust pastry, line this with parchment paper and pie weights or dried beans, and bake for 15 minutes. Remove the weights and paper. Whisk 3 eggs with ¾ cup light cream and 1 tablespoon chopped tarragon. Season well. Stir in 3 skinned, deseeded, and diced tomatoes. Spoon into the pastry case and bake for 25 minutes, or until just set.

6

Tomato and spinach dhal

Bring 1¼ cups rinsed red lentils and 4 cups water to a boil in a large pan and simmer for 10 minutes. Add one 14 oz can plum tomatoes, ½ teaspoon ground turmeric, 1½ inch piece ginger (grated), 2 crushed garlic cloves, 1 teaspoon cumin seeds, and 2 chopped green chilies. Stir, then simmer gently for 15–20 minutes, stirring often. Fold in 4½ cups young leaf spinach, a squeeze of lime juice, and salt and pepper. Eat warm with steamed rice or Indian flatbread.

5

Cherry tomato tarte tatin

Preheat the oven to 375°F (Gas 5). Place a 6 inch ovenproof frying pan over low heat and add 2 tablespoons olive oil, heaping scant ½ cup superfine sugar, and 1⅔ cups whole cherry tomatoes. Fry until the sugar caramelizes to a deep golden color, then add 2 tablespoons balsamic vinegar. Remove from the heat and season. Tuck 7 inch circle of rolled-out puff pastry over and around the tomatoes and bake for about 15 minutes until the pastry is cooked. Carefully turn out onto a plate while still warm and serve with spoonfuls of the walnut tarator on page 241.

One-Pots
and Bakes
Chapter Seven

The grated parsnip gradually melts into the rice in this buttery but light risotto. A couple of fried sage leaves will elevate this into posh dinner territory. You could go one further with parsnip chips: slice parsnips very thin with a vegetable peeler, coat in olive oil, and roast at 325°F (Gas 2–3) for 25–30 minutes, turning halfway, until crisp.

Parsnip, sage, and mascarpone risotto

SERVES 4
PREPARATION TIME: 10 MINUTES
COOKING TIME: 25 MINUTES

4 cups vegetable stock (see page 236) or good-quality bought stock

3 tablespoons butter

2 shallots, finely chopped

2 large parsnips, coarsely grated

4 small sage leaves, finely shredded

1⅓ cups risotto rice, ideally Vialone Nano

⅓ cup dry white wine

2 tablespoons mascarpone, plus extra to serve

2¼ oz Parmesan, finely grated

parsnip crisps, to serve (optional)

Pour the vegetable stock into a saucepan and bring it up to simmering point. Reduce the heat to low to keep the stock hot.

In another pan, melt the butter and add the shallots, parsnips, and sage. Cook gently, stirring, for 5 minutes until the shallots are soft but not colored. Stir in the rice to coat thoroughly with the buttery vegetables and cook for a minute. Pour in the wine and stir until it evaporates, then start adding the hot stock, a ladleful at a time, stirring after each addition of stock until it virtually disappears. Continue this process for 18–20 minutes, or until the rice grains are plump but retain a bit of "bite" and the risotto is creamy. You may not need all the stock.

Remove from the heat and swirl in half the mascarpone and grated Parmesan. Cover and set aside for 5 minutes. Mix the remaining cheeses through and serve with an extra spoonful of mascarpone on top, with a scattering of parsnip chips (if using).

This is a cunning way to cook pizza at a very high temperature, and hotter than most domestic ovens will allow. By doing it this way, the already-grilled crust gets even crisper and pleasingly charred as the cheese melts—and you don't need to buy your own pizza oven.

Grilled vegetable pizza

SERVES 2–4
PREPARATION TIME: 20 MINUTES
PLUS RESTING TIME
COOKING TIME: 15 MINUTES

FOR THE PIZZA BASE:

1⅔ cups white bread flour

½ teaspoon rapid-rise dry yeast

¾ teaspoon salt

2 tablespoons extra virgin olive oil, plus extra to oil the bowl

¾ cup lukewarm water

FOR THE TOPPING:

2 small zucchini, very finely sliced

1 fennel bulb, finely sliced

4 rosemary sprigs, leaves stripped

2 tablespoons extra virgin olive oil

2 tablespoons polenta or cornmeal

2 balls buffalo mozzarella, torn into pieces

Start by making the dough for the pizza base. Combine the dry ingredients in a large mixing bowl and add the olive oil as well as enough of the warm water to form a soft, shaggy dough. Use a wooden spoon and then your hands to blend the mixture. Turn out onto a clean, lightly floured surface and knead for 10 minutes until the dough is smooth, elastic, and bouncy. Oil the bowl and return the dough to it, then cover with a clean, damp dishtowel and leave in a warm place for an hour.

Meanwhile, preheat the broiler. Coat the vegetables and rosemary in a little olive oil and season well. Spread out in an oiled baking tray and broil for about 4 minutes, turning halfway. Set aside but keep the broiler on. Ensure the shelf is at the top and close to the heating element.

Place a very sturdy, large frying pan over high heat—a thick, cast-iron pan is ideal. Leave it on the burner for at least 10 minutes, as it needs to get smoking hot.

Knock the dough back to let the air out, divide it in half, and gently press and stretch each piece into a rough circle, a little bit smaller than your hot pan. It should be thin—about ¼ inch. Lay each circle of dough on a sheet of parchment paper sprinkled with a tablespoon of polenta or cornmeal. Cover the pizza bases with the broiled vegetables and the torn mozzarella, then drizzle with a little olive oil.

Slide one of the pizzas off the paper and into the smoking hot pan. Leave for a minute, then transfer the pan to the hot broiler (you'll need oven gloves!) and cook for about 4 minutes. Slide the pizza onto a cutting board and place the pan back on high heat while you slice the cooked pizza into wedges. Cook the second pizza in the same way while you eat the first.

These light and fluffy little parcels don't have to be baked—you could serve them straightaway with the melted herb butter or perhaps the Gorgonzola sauce on page 240. All you'll need to accompany them is a crisp salad, which will cut through the buttery richness.

Ricotta gnocchi gratin with parsley butter

SERVES 4
PREPARATION TIME: 30 MINUTES
PLUS DRAINING TIME
COOKING TIME: 13–18 MINUTES

1 lb ricotta

2 eggs, beaten

1 tablespoon butter, melted

a few gratings of nutmeg

⅓ heaping cup Parmesan, finely grated

about ⅔ cup all-purpose flour, plus extra for dusting

⅓ cup parsley butter (see page 234), diced

It's very important to drain the ricotta thoroughly so try to do this the day before. Line a colander with cheesecloth and lay the ricotta in it. Set over a bowl, cover, and leave to drain for 8–24 hours. Alternatively, put the ricotta in several layers of cheesecloth and gather up into a ball. Squeeze firmly to force the water out. Place the cheese in a colander and weigh it down with a small plate and a couple of unopened cans to force more water out. Set aside for 20 minutes, then wring out again before you unwrap it. Turn the drained cheese into a bowl and mash with a fork. Add the eggs, butter, nutmeg, and ½ oz of the Parmesan. Season with salt and pepper, then fork through to mix lightly but evenly.

Measure the flour onto a plate. Drop heaped teaspoonfuls of the ricotta mixture into the flour—do them in batches of about 5 or so. Turn them over with a fork, then fish the bundles out one by one and gently jiggle each of them in your hand to form lightly floured ovals. Don't squeeze or press. Place on a lightly floured tray and repeat. You can cook the gnocchi straightaway or chill for an hour or so to firm them.

Put half the parsley butter in a heatproof bowl and preheat the oven to 400°F (Gas 6). Bring a large, wide pot of generously salted water to a simmer, drop in the gnocchi one by one, and cook until they float to the surface—this will take about 3 minutes. Remove the gnocchi from the pan with a slotted spoon, shaking excess water off, and drop them into the bowl of parsley butter. Toss gently to melt the butter, then tip into a medium gratin dish. Dot with the remaining parsley butter cubes and shower with the rest of the grated Parmesan. Bake for 10–15 minutes until golden and bubbling. Serve with a simple green salad.

Toasting before steaming or simmering adds a whole new dimension to couscous. The main thing to bear in mind is that you must season it generously. Herbs, citrus zest, spices, and good olive oil will also give the toasted grain a nudge along in the flavor stakes.

Baked red onions stuffed with toasted, spiced couscous

SERVES 4
PREPARATION TIME: 20 MINUTES
COOKING TIME: 1 HOUR 40 MINUTES

4 large red onions, skins on

2 tablespoons olive oil, plus extra for drizzling

2 tablespoons butter

½ teaspoon ground cinnamon

3 tablespoons uncooked couscous

1¼ cups vegetable stock (see page 236) or good-quality bought stock

2 tablespoons chopped dried apricots

2 tablespoons pine nuts, toasted in a dry pan

1 tablespoon chopped flat-leaf parsley

Preheat the oven to 400°F (Gas 6). Cut the tops off the onions and reserve. Slice any fibers off the root ends of the onions so they can sit upright, but leave as intact as possible so the onions hold together. Place in a baking dish or casserole, pour in ⅓ cup water, and drizzle with olive oil. Cover with foil or a lid and bake for 1 hour, then uncover and set aside. When just cool enough to handle, scoop out the onion centers with a teaspoon, leaving enough outside layers to form a thick shell. Roughly chop the scooped-out flesh.

Heat the 2 tablespoons of olive oil and 1 tablespoon of the butter in a frying pan. Add the chopped, scooped-out onion plus the cinnamon and couscous. Stir for a few minutes until the couscous turns golden. Add ½ cup stock, season generously with salt and pepper, and remove from the heat. Set aside for 5 minutes, then add the apricots, pine nuts, and parsley and mix well.

Spoon this mixture into the hollowed-out onions in the cooking dish, and pop the onion tops into the dish as well, along with the remaining stock. Dot with the remaining 1 tablespoon butter and bake uncovered for 25 minutes until golden. Cover the onions with foil or a lid if the tops brown too much before the cooking time is up. Perch the tops back on the onions to serve if you like.

Chestnuts aren't just for Christmas, although this would make a very good Yuletide side dish. Waxy potatoes or chunks of celery root or parsnip can replace the Jerusalem artichokes if you prefer.

Braised, buttered chestnuts with Jerusalem artichokes

SERVES 3–4
PREPARATION TIME: 15 MINUTES
COOKING TIME: 30 MINUTES

1 lb 2 oz Jerusalem artichokes

a squeeze of lemon

¼ cup butter

1 sweet white onion, finely sliced

2 garlic cloves, unpeeled and bruised

4 bay leaves

2 cups cooked and peeled chestnuts (vacuum-packed are fine)

⅓ cup red wine

⅓ cup vegetable stock (see page 236) or good-quality bought stock

Start by peeling the Jerusalem artichokes. Cut them into ¾ inch slices and submerge in a bowlful of cold water spiked with a squeeze of lemon.

Melt the butter in a large casserole or deep-sided frying pan and add the onion. Cook gently for 5 minutes until softened. Add the garlic cloves, bay leaves, and thoroughly drained artichokes, followed by the chestnuts and a little salt and pepper. Stir to coat the vegetables in the butter. Cover the pan and cook for 10 minutes, stirring occasionally. Then add the wine and stock, and bring to a boil. Simmer for 10 minutes, or until the artichokes are tender and the liquid reduced. Check the seasoning.

You can use a fork to crush the sweet and mild cooked garlic cloves into the sauce before serving to add body and depth. There won't be any hint of harsh garlic flavor—just fish out and discard the papery skin.

Serve with steamed greens and perhaps some pureed potatoes if you are particularly hungry.

 One-Pots and Bakes

Undercooked eggplants are disappointing indeed, but there's little chance of that happening here. Fried until crisp and golden, then braised, these are silky smooth and tender—just as they should be.

Braised baby eggplant with bok choy, peanuts, and Thai basil

SERVES 4
PREPARATION TIME: 15 MINUTES
COOKING TIME: 10–15 MINUTES

scant ½ cup peanut oil

12 baby eggplants, halved

2 garlic cloves, chopped

1¼ inch piece ginger, finely chopped

6 heads baby bok choy, halved

4 spring onions, sliced

2 tablespoons light soy sauce

2 teaspoons palm sugar or light brown sugar

3 tablespoons peanuts, toasted and crushed

a small handful of Thai basil leaves

Score the flesh of the eggplants in a crisscross pattern, then heat the oil in a large wok until it shimmers. Add the eggplants and fry, turning with tongs, until deeply golden. Remove to a plate lined with paper towels then carefully pour most of the oil out of the wok, leaving about a tablespoonful behind.

Return the wok to the heat and add the garlic and ginger. Stir-fry for half a minute, then add the bok choy and spring onions. Continue to stir-fry for a minute or so more.

Return the eggplants to the wok with the soy sauce, plus the palm or brown sugar and 2 tablespoons water. Allow to bubble and thicken for a couple more minutes.

Scatter with crushed peanuts and Thai basil and serve with steamed rice.

This Malaysian egg curry is fragrant and feisty, requiring only steamed rice to serve. Traditionally, the eggs would be hard-boiled, but this dish is far more delicious when they're a little soft inside. To soft-boil eggs, cover them with cold water in a saucepan and place over medium heat. As soon as the water boils, remove from the heat and set aside for seven minutes. Refresh in cool water and peel carefully.

Sambal Telur

SERVES 4
PREPARATION TIME: 15 MINUTES
COOKING TIME: 15 MINUTES

3 vine-ripened tomatoes

1 tablespoon peanut oil

4 shallots, finely sliced

3 garlic cloves, chopped

1½ inch piece ginger, finely chopped

1 teaspoon coriander seeds, crushed

1 teaspoon cumin seeds, crushed

½ teaspoon ground turmeric

1 tablespoon sambal oelek

one 14 fl oz can coconut milk

2 tablespoons tamarind pulp

1 tablespoon palm sugar or brown sugar

8 eggs, soft-boiled

2 tablespoons fried shallots, to serve

Cut a shallow cross in the base of the tomatoes with a sharp knife and place them in a bowl. Cover with boiling water and leave for a minute. Drain and peel, then roughly chop the flesh and set aside.

Heat the oil in a wok or saucepan, add the shallots, garlic, and ginger, and cook for a minute. Add the coriander, cumin, turmeric, sambal oelek, and the chopped tomatoes and sauté for a few minutes more.

Stir in the coconut milk, tamarind pulp, and palm sugar along with a hefty pinch of salt. Bring to the boil and simmer for 5 minutes until the mixture thickens.

Add the eggs and simmer for a few more minutes to heat them through. Scatter with fried shallots and serve the curry with steamed rice.

Side dishes

2

Green papaya salad

Peel a large green papaya and shred the flesh. Add to a bowl with 1 large shredded carrot and dress with a few tablespoons of ginger and lime dipping sauce (see page 244). Toss through a couple of spoonfuls of Thai basil leaves, and top with chopped, toasted peanuts or cashews.

Greens dressed with walnut tarator

Plunge some seasonal greens—any type of kale or cabbage, broccoli, chard, or bok choy—into salted water and simmer until just tender. Drain and dress the vegetables with walnut tarator (see page 241).

Asparagus with brioche crumbs

Cook trimmed green asparagus spears in salted water until just tender. Melt a generous lump of butter in a frying pan and add finely processed brioche crumbs with the grated zest of ½ lemon. Stir and toast until golden. Season and scatter over the drained asparagus. You could also serve the cooked asparagus with blender hollandaise or Gorgonzola sauce (see page 240).

3

4

Red cabbage slaw with gomashio

Slice ½ medium red cabbage very finely and finely slice a quartered, cored red apple. Dress with a little toasted sesame oil, rice vinegar, and soy sauce. Toss through a few cilantro leaves and scatter with gomashio (see page 236). This also goes splendidly with grilled corn or shredded carrot.

5

Beet and fig carpaccio with tapenade dressing

Slice 4 raw peeled beets into paper-thin slices and slice 3 ripe figs as thinly as you can without the flesh breaking. Place on a plate and scatter with a few lemon thyme leaves. Combine 2 tablespoons fig tapenade (see page 240) with 1 tablespoon red wine vinegar, 1 tablespoon extra virgin olive oil, and 1 tablespoon water. Spoon over the beets and figs and season lightly to finish.

6

Spiced sweet potato wedges

Preheat the oven to 400°F (Gas 6). Peel 1½ lb sweet potatoes, or leave the skin on if you wish, and slice into wedges. Toss the wedges in 3 tablespoons olive oil, 2 crushed garlic cloves, 1 tablespoon each crushed cumin, fennel, and coriander seeds, and a pinch of dried chili flakes. Season and spread cut on a baking tray. Bake for 35 minutes or so, turning halfway. Serve the potatoes as they are or with parsley or arugula pesto (see page 238).

Sometimes only a comforting, familiar supper will do. Make the whole thing in advance to reheat when needed if you wish, or just pre-make the crêpes. Stack them, each one separated by parchment paper, and keep well-wrapped in the refrigerator for a day or two.

Spinach, herb, and ricotta crêpes gratin

SERVES 4
PREPARATION TIME: 20 MINUTES
PLUS STANDING TIME
COOKING TIME: ABOUT 30 MINUTES

FOR THE CRÊPES:

1 cup plus 2 tablespoons milk

2 eggs, beaten

2 tablespoons butter, melted, plus a little extra to cook the crêpes

⅓ heaping cup whole wheat flour

½ cup buckwheat flour

FOR THE FILLING:

2 tablespoons butter, plus extra for greasing

4½ cups spinach leaves, washed and dried

1 heaping cup ricotta, drained

2 tablespoons roughly chopped soft herbs, such as chives, basil, or parsley

a good grating of nutmeg

4 tablespoons finely grated Parmesan

1 quantity rustic, slow-roasted tomato sauce (see page 242)

1 ball buffalo mozzarella, torn into pieces

Start with the crêpes. Whisk the milk, eggs, and butter into the flours with a pinch of salt to make a smooth batter, or process the ingredients briefly in a blender. Transfer to a bowl and, if you have time, leave the batter to stand for 20 minutes or so. Place a medium frying pan over medium-high heat and add a small lump of butter. When it melts and sizzles, pour a small ladleful (about 2 tablespoons) of stirred batter into the pan and swirl to cover the base completely so you form a thin crêpe. Allow to cook for a minute or so, then flip and cook for a minute more. Slide onto a plate and repeat to make 8 pancakes. Stack the cooked crêpes on top of each other, separated by squares of parchment paper to stop them sticking.

Grease a large gratin dish and preheat the oven to 400°F (Gas 6).

To make the filling, wilt the spinach in the butter and remove from the heat. Once cooled a little, roughly chop the spinach and stir into the ricotta with the herbs, nutmeg, and half the Parmesan. Spoon an eighth of the mixture onto the center of each crêpe and fold in half, then in half again, to form a fan shape. Place the filled crêpes in the buttered gratin dish and spoon the tomato sauce over. Scatter with the remaining Parmesan and the torn mozzarella and bake for 20 minutes or so until the cheese is golden and bubbling.

This is nourishing comfort food at its finest. It's a meltingly delicious dish, which has an appealingly sweet combination of flavors that children love, but the addition of some waxy potato would temper it a little. Of course, feel free to vary the root vegetables as you wish.

Shredded root vegetable gratin with crème fraîche and Gruyère

SERVES 4–6
PREPARATION TIME: 20 MINUTES
COOKING TIME: 40 MINUTES

1 garlic clove, halved

soft butter, for greasing

4 cups coarsely grated butternut squash or pumpkin

2 cups firmly packed grated carrot

2 cups firmly packed grated parsnip

2 cups firmly packed grated sweet potato

1⅔ cups crème fraîche

scant ½ cup dry white wine

1¼ cups coarsely grated Gruyère

2 teaspoons thyme leaves

Preheat the oven to 400°F (Gas 6). Rub the cut garlic around the inside of a deep, medium-sized gratin dish. Discard the garlic clove and smear the dish with butter.

Place half the shredded vegetables in the dish, pressing them down firmly to expel as much air as possible. You can keep the vegetable layers distinct or mix all the varieties together, as you wish. Either way, season the layers well with salt and pepper.

Mix the crème fraîche and wine together and season with salt and pepper. Spoon half this mixture over the vegetables and top with about ⅓ cup of the grated Gruyère. Scatter half the thyme over, and top with the remaining vegetables, pressing down firmly as before. Pour the remaining crème fraîche mixture over, scatter with a little salt, pepper, and the remaining thyme, and finish with the last remaining Gruyère.

Cover with foil, seal well, and bake for 30 minutes. Uncover, then bake for a further 30 minutes or so until golden and bubbling. Let the gratin rest and settle for at least 10 minutes before serving with a salad or steamed green vegetables.

This is a stunning, rustic starter. Should the idea of preparing fresh artichokes instill fear in your heart, don't worry, you can use the deli-style artichoke halves in oil. If you do, simply sauté the shallots and garlic, and stir in the other stuffing ingredients before spooning into the artichokes and baking for 15–20 minutes to brown. You won't need the stock.

Artichokes with lemon and oregano bread crumbs and citrus mayonnaise

SERVES 4
PREPARATION TIME: 30 MINUTES
COOKING TIME: ABOUT 50 MINUTES

FOR THE ARTICHOKES:

12 young violet artichokes

finely grated zest and juice of 1 lemon

2 shallots, finely chopped

4 tablespoons olive oil

1 garlic clove, crushed

1⅔ cups (lightly packed) coarse sourdough bread crumbs

1 tablespoon oregano leaves, chopped

⅓ cup white wine

⅓ cup vegetable stock (see page 236) or good-quality bought stock

FOR THE MAYONNAISE:

½ quantity mayonnaise (see page 236) or ½ cup good-quality bought mayonnaise

finely grated zest of 1 lemon

1 tablespoon lemon juice

Preheat the oven to 350°F (Gas 4). Slice off the stalks from the artichokes so they will stand upright. Remove the tough outer leaves from each artichoke bud until you reach the lighter-colored leaves beneath. Cut the spiny tops off the leaves, open the leaves out slightly, and use a teaspoon to scoop out the hairy central core or choke, and discard. Drop the prepared artichokes into a bowl of cold water with the lemon juice added.

In a casserole or sturdy roasting pan, soften the shallots in 3 tablespoons olive oil until translucent. Add the garlic and cook for another minute. Scoop the mixture into a bowl and add the bread crumbs, lemon zest, and oregano along with some salt and pepper. Mix well. Remove the artichokes from the water and shake them dry. Spoon the stuffing mixture into the cavities between the leaves.

Add the remaining oil to the same casserole or pan and sit the artichokes in it. Pour in the wine and stock and cover tightly with a lid or a double layer of foil. Bake for 30 minutes, then uncover and cook for a further 10–15 minutes until the bread crumbs are golden.

Stir the lemon zest and juice into the mayonnaise and serve alongside the artichokes.

A French variation on Italian pizza, this sharply savory tart is traditionally crisscrossed with salty anchovies. Clearly, this would not be the vegetarian way to go, so anchovies have been replaced by scarlet strips of sun-dried tomato—with anything but ill effect.

Pissaladière

SERVES 4–6
PREPARATION TIME: 35 MINUTES
PLUS CHILLING TIME
COOKING TIME: ABOUT 1 HOUR

FOR THE FILLING:

2 lb onions, finely sliced

3 tablespoons olive oil

3 14 oz cans plum tomatoes, drained and roughly chopped

18 sun-dried tomatoes in oil, drained and sliced into strips

12 black olives, pitted

FOR THE PASTRY:

1¼ cups all-purpose flour

½ teaspoon salt

⅓ cup butter, cubed

1 egg yolk

2–3 tablespoons iced water

a little flour, for dusting

Soften the onions in the olive oil in a large saucepan. Keep the heat low and the lid on the pan; the onions must not over-brown or burn at this stage, so check them often and stir regularly. When they are a pale golden color—about 30 minutes later—remove the lid and add the chopped plum tomatoes. Turn the heat up a little and continue to cook until any liquid has evaporated and the tomatoes have started to break down.

Next, make the pastry. Place the flour, salt, and butter in a food processor and pulse until the mixture is finely blended—but don't overwork it. Add the egg yolk and 2 tablespoons iced water and pulse again, adding more water by the teaspoonful until the pastry comes together to form a ball.

Preheat the oven to 375°F (Gas 5). Roll out the pastry on a lightly floured surface and transfer to a 14 x 4½ inch rectangular or 8 inch round tart pan. Press the pastry in firmly to fit, but make sure not to stretch it or it will shrink while baking. Leave the sides untrimmed, prick the base lightly with a fork, and chill for 30 minutes.

When chilled, cover the pastry shell with parchment paper and fill with pie weights or dried beans. Bake for 10 minutes, then remove the paper and beans and cook for another 5 minutes or so until the pastry turns a very pale gold. Remove the pastry shell from the oven and, once it has cooled a little, trim the edges flush with the pan using a very sharp knife.

Fill the pastry shell with the onion mixture, pressing it out evenly. Use the strips of sun-dried tomato to make a crisscross pattern on top and stud the gaps with black olives. Bake for 20–25 minutes. Cover the tart with a loose sheet of foil if the pastry seems to be browning too quickly.

The ingredients are rich, but this is a delicate dish that's elegant rather than clumsy, thanks to fine layering. As with all simple food, it demands quality ingredients. Ideally, make lasagne sheets from the pasta recipe on page 216, multiplying the quantities by 1.5. Or use sheets of good-quality bought fresh pasta, and roll them out ethereally thin.

Fine white lasagne with many layers

SERVES 6–8
PREPARATION TIME: 40 MINUTES
PLUS INFUSING TIME
COOKING TIME: 50 MINUTES

1 quantity Béchamel sauce
(see page 241)

butter for greasing

1 lb fresh lasagne sheets

olive oil, for dizzling

10½ oz mushrooms, any sort,
finely chopped

2 tablespoons butter

1 garlic clove, crushed

a large handful of basil leaves

4 tablespoons finely grated Parmesan

2 balls buffalo mozzarella,
torn into pieces

Start by making the Béchamel sauce, then cover to prevent a skin forming and set aside.

Preheat the oven to 350°F (Gas 4) and grease a medium-large ceramic lasagne dish. Cut the lasagne sheets into halves or thirds so they can be layered in the dish easily. Drop each sheet, one by one, into a pot of boiling, salted water. Simmer for a mere minute or two, then drain and refresh under cold running water. Drizzle with olive oil and lay the sheets out on clean dishtowels in a single layer.

Sauté the mushrooms gently in the butter for a few minutes until softened but not colored. Stir in the garlic and cook for a further 2 minutes until much of the liquid has cooked off. Spread a little of the mixture over the base of the dish and scatter with basil leaves. Don't use much; this is all about fine and delicate layering, not thick bands of filling. Cover the mushrooms with a layer of pasta, a very thin layer of Béchamel, a little seasoning, and a meager sprinkle of Parmesan. Top with another layer of pasta, then begin the layering process again, starting with the mushrooms. Continue layering like this until you have used all the ingredients, finishing with lasagne sheets, Béchamel sauce, and a final layer of torn mozzarella, all dusted with some grated Parmesan.

Bake for 35 minutes or so until the lasagne is bubbling and golden at the edges.

This frittata makes a perfect supper: it's easy to prepare and allows you to put your feet up while it bakes to firmness in the oven. The barley, an unusual inclusion in frittata, is cooked until tender but still chewy. If you prefer it softer, simmer it for an extra 10 minutes.

Oven-baked pea, barley, and fava bean frittata

SERVES 6
PREPARATION TIME: 15 MINUTES
COOKING TIME: 50 MINUTES

¾ cup pearl barley

2 mint sprigs

⅔ cup shelled peas

½ cup fava beans, pods and skins removed

6 eggs, lightly beaten

3 tablespoons heavy cream

1 garlic clove, crushed

3 tablespoons olive oil

1 heaping cup cubed halloumi

Cover the barley with plenty of cold water. Add a pinch of salt and a sprig of mint, and bring to a boil. Simmer for 20 minutes until the barley is tender. Add the peas and fava beans and simmer for a few minutes more, then drain.

Preheat the oven to 400°F (Gas 6). Chop the remaining mint leaves and add to the eggs with the cream and crushed garlic. Season with plenty of pepper but only a little salt because the cheese is salty. Place a large, ovenproof frying pan over medium heat and add the olive oil. Spoon the barley mixture into the pan and spread it out. Pour in the egg mixture, shaking the frying pan to distribute it evenly, and then scatter with the halloumi, pushing some of it down into the egg. Cook for a couple of minutes, then pop the pan into the oven for 15–20 minutes to set the egg and brown the cheese. Rest the frittata for 5 minutes before slicing and serving.

Risottos

Zucchini and Taleggio

Make the basic risotto bianco, but stir in a few thyme leaves and 2 trimmed and finely diced zucchini about 15 minutes into the rice cooking time. When the grains are just cooked, fold in 1 cup diced Taleggio with the butter and Parmesan, and set aside to rest. The cheese cubes will become molten and voluptuous as they warm through.

Bianco

Heat 4 cups vegetable stock. Soften 3 finely chopped shallots in 1 tablespoon olive oil and 1 tablespoon butter. Add 1¾ cups risotto rice and stir to coat the rice in buttery oil. Add 1 cup dry white wine. Stir until evaporated, then add a pinch of salt and a ladleful of stock. Stir. As the stock evaporates, add more and stir, continuing for about 18 minutes until the rice is just tender. Remove from heat and stir in 3 tablespoons cubed butter and 1 cup finely grated Parmesan. Cover and set aside for 2 minutes before serving.

Tomato and pesto

Make the basic risotto bianco but stir in 12 roughly chopped slow-roasted tomato halves (see page 242) halfway through cooking the rice. Omit the butter at the end and stir in only ½ cup grated Parmesan. Serve each bowlful topped with a spoonful of classic pesto (see page 238), an extra roasted tomato half, and scatter with extra basil leaves.

4

Fennel and lemon

Make the basic risotto bianco but include a large, finely chopped fennel bulb and a finely chopped garlic clove with the shallots. Five minutes before the end of cooking, stir in the finely grated zest of a lemon. When the risotto is cooked, add the juice of a small lemon and replace the 3 tablespoons butter with 3 tablespoons mascarpone. Finish with chopped fennel tops and a grating of lemon zest.

6

Cauliflower pangrattato

Make the basic risotto bianco but add 3¼ cups cauliflower florets and a bay leaf to the stock. Simmer for 10 minutes. Add 2 crushed garlic cloves to the shallots and, when adding stock to the rice, include the cauliflower. Process 5½ oz sourdough bread with a pinch of dried chili flakes, a garlic clove, and 1 teaspoon thyme leaves until crumbs form. Fry with 2 tablespoons butter and 2 tablespoons olive oil until golden. Serve the risotto scattered with the toasted crumbs.

5

Wild garlic

Make the basic risotto bianco and, just a couple of minutes before the rice is cooked, stir in about 3 cups wild garlic leaves. Add the butter and cheese and continue the risotto bianco recipe as written. Serve with extra Parmesan.

Special

Chapter Eight

Eggplant caviar is also known as "poor man's caviar," but that's a misnomer. True, you won't find a single fish egg here, but this is still a luxurious mouthful to serve as a canapé, or before a special dinner. And with its pomegranate jewels, it's as pretty as a picture.

Chervil pancakes with eggplant caviar and pomegranate

MAKES ABOUT 24
PREPARATION TIME: 15 MINUTES
PLUS COOLING TIME
COOKING TIME: 1 HOUR

FOR THE EGGPLANT CAVIAR:

1 garlic clove

1 teaspoon cumin seeds

2 medium eggplants, halved lengthwise

3 tablespoons extra virgin olive oil

2 teaspoons pomegranate molasses or a squeeze of lemon

4 tablespoons thick Greek yogurt

3 tablespoons fresh pomegranate seeds

FOR THE PANCAKES:

1½ cups self-rising flour

1 teaspoon baking powder

2 eggs, beaten

1 cup buttermilk

1 tablespoon chopped chervil, plus extra leaves to serve

butter, for greasing

Preheat the oven to 400°F (Gas 6). Use a mortar and pestle to crush the garlic with the cumin seeds and a large pinch of salt. Spread this mixture over the cut surfaces of the eggplants, then sandwich the halves together and wrap in foil. Bake for 40 minutes until tender, then unwrap and set aside to cool.

With a spoon, scoop the flesh from the eggplants into a saucepan and discard the skins. Add the olive oil and heat the pan, stirring the mixture as it simmers. Cook for 5 minutes or so to evaporate the excess water and concentrate the flavors. Leave to cool, then beat in the pomegranate molasses or lemon juice, a tablespoon of yogurt, and a little salt and pepper to taste.

Combine 2 tablespoons of the pomegranate seeds with the remaining yogurt and set aside.

To make the pancakes, whisk all the ingredients together, except the extra chervil leaves, until smooth. Cook heaped teaspoonfuls of the mixture in a hot frying pan greased with the butter. They will take a minute or two on each side to cook. Flip them when the little bubbles that rise to the surface start to burst.

Place a teaspoonful of the eggplant mixture on each pancake and top with a little yogurt. Add a few pomegranate seeds and a sprig of chervil to finish.

Special

Stéphane Reynaud has been chef-proprietor of Villa9trois in Montreuil, near Paris, since 2003. His recipes combine his enthusiasm for modern cuisine with his passion for the freshest, best-quality seasonal produce. He favors these wonderful spring rolls for their simplicity, and because they can be adapted with the seasons. In winter, try using Stilton, pears, beets, mâche, … and so on.

Stéphane Reynaud's
Summer spring rolls

SERVES 6
PREPARATION TIME: 30 MINUTES

FOR THE TOMATO COULIS:

4 large, very ripe tomatoes

a little olive oil

1½ inch piece ginger, grated

1 small onion, finely chopped

4 garlic cloves, finely chopped

1 spring onion, finely chopped

FOR THE ROLLS:

7 oz fresh, soft goat cheese

2 tablespoons olive oil

6 large or 12 small rice paper rounds

1 mango, peeled, pitted, and sliced into matchsticks

1½ cups soy sprouts

¾ cup afalfa sprouts

½ cucumber, peeled, deseeded, and sliced into matchsticks

a handful of arugula leaves

2 tablespoons soy sauce

Start with the tomato coulis. Cut a cross in the base of the tomatoes, cover with boiling water in a bowl, and leave for 30 seconds. Drain, remove the skins, and roughly chop. Pour a little olive oil into a saucepan and soften the ginger, onion, and garlic over medium heat until golden. Add the peeled tomatoes and cook gently for 20 minutes. Purée in a blender until smooth, and season to taste. Set aside until ready to serve, or keep in the refrigerator for up to 3 days.

To make the rolls, mix the chopped spring onion with the goat cheese and olive oil. Spoon into a piping bag fitted with a large, straight nozzle. Place a clean, damp dishtowel flat on your work surface. Soak one rice paper round at a time in lukewarm water to soften, place it on the towel, and pipe a line of cheese paste along the horizontal "edge" nearest you. Pile one-twelfth or one-sixth (depending on whether your rice paper rounds are small or large, respectively) of the mango and vegetables along this line. Fold in the vertical sides by ½ inch and roll tightly away from you. Repeat until all the rice paper rounds are full.

To serve, halve the rolls (if small) or cut into four pieces (if large), and drop a little soy sauce onto each. Serve with tomato coulis.

Miang kham are traditional Thai snacks, and here these delicious parcels have been repackaged slightly to become fresh and elegant canapés or starters. Betel leaves are widely used in cooking and for medicinal purposes throughout Southeast Asia.

Betel leaf wraps with coconut and cashews

MAKES 20
PREPARATION TIME: 20 MINUTES
COOKING TIME: ABOUT 10 MINUTES

1¾ oz fresh or dried shredded coconut, toasted

1½ inch piece ginger, finely chopped

2 Thai chilies, finely chopped

3 tablespoons chopped cashews, toasted

¾ cup, firmly packed palm sugar or light brown soft sugar

¼ cup vegetarian fish sauce or soy sauce

2 tablespoons sieved tamarind pulp or tamarind purée

½ small lime, finely diced, including skin

1 small pomelo, flesh separated and pulled into small chunks

1 shallot, finely chopped

20 betel leaves or spinach leaves

a handful of coriander sprouts or cilantro sprigs

Using a mortar and pestle or a mini food processor, grind to a paste half the coconut, half the ginger, the chilies and 2 tablespoons cashews with a pinch of salt. Set aside.

Combine the palm or brown sugar with ¼ cup water in a saucepan and heat gently until dissolved. Increase the heat and simmer for a few minutes until reduced to syrup. Stir in the pounded paste with the vegetarian fish sauce or soy sauce. Simmer for 3 minutes more and stir in the tamarind. Heat through, then remove from the heat. Cool a little.

Mix together the lime, pomelo, and shallot. Place teaspoonfuls of this mixture onto the center of the betel leaves, shiny sides down, and add a little of the cooled tamarind mixture, followed by a couple coriander sprouts or cilantro sprigs. Pinch each leaf together slightly at the base. You can use a small cocktail pick to secure them if you like.

Special

Skye Gyngell is head chef at Petersham Nurseries Cafe in Richmond, southwest of London, a restaurant famed for its beautiful surroundings and inventive seasonal food. To make the vibrant basil oil in this recipe, process the leaves from 3 large bunches of basil, 1 peeled garlic clove, and a good pinch each of salt and pepper. With the motor running, trickle in ¾ cup plus 1 tablespoon of extra virgin olive oil.

Skye Gyngell's

Nectarine and tomato salad with buffalo mozzarella

SERVES 4
PREPARATION TIME: 15 MINUTES

4 perfectly ripe nectarines

12 perfectly ripe heirloom tomatoes

a few drops of lemon juice

2 tablespoons good-quality extra virgin olive oil

sea salt and freshly ground black pepper

4 balls of buffalo mozzarella

12 purple basil leaves, torn or shredded

2 tablespoons basil oil (see introduction above)

aged balsamic vinegar, to drizzle (optional)

Cut the nectarines in half along their natural division, remove the stones and cut each half into 3 wedges. Halve the tomatoes. Place the nectarines and tomatoes in a bowl and sprinkle with a few drops of lemon juice. Drizzle over the extra virgin olive oil and season with a little salt and pepper.

Tear the mozzarella balls in half with your fingers and lay 2 halves on each plate. Now build your salad, alternating the peach slices and tomatoes with basil, spooning a little basil oil between the layers and seasoning delicately as you go. Finish with a restrained drizzle of balsamic vinegar, if you like. Serve at once, preferably with really good chewy peasant-style bread drizzled with more olive oil.

White asparagus is grown in darkness below the soil surface to keep it blanched of color, and the resulting spears are delicately flavored. Some people add sugar to the cooking water to prevent bitterness, but simmering them in diluted milk has the same effect and won't taint the vegetable with unnecessary sweetness.

White asparagus with Champagne beurre blanc

SERVES 4
PREPARATION TIME: 10 MINUTES
COOKING TIME: 20 MINUTES

FOR THE BEURRE BLANC:

1 shallot, finely chopped

4 black peppercorns

1 tarragon sprig

¾ cup Champagne or dry white wine

¾ cup butter, chilled and cubed

FOR THE ASPARAGUS:

20 white asparagus spears, about 1¼ lb

¾ cup plus 1 tablespoon milk

1 tablespoon butter

Start by making the beurre blanc reduction. Place the shallot, peppercorns, tarragon, and Champagne or dry white wine in a saucepan and bring to a boil. Simmer the liquid down slowly for a few minutes until reduced by two-thirds. Strain through a sieve into a heatproof bowl.

Trim the tough ¾ inch or so from the base of each asparagus spear. Carefully pare away the skin from the stalks (but not the tips) using a vegetable peeler, treating them gently so the spears don't snap.

Using a frying pan large enough to hold the stalks in a single layer, lay the asparagus out flat. Add the milk and ½ oz butter with ¾ cup plus 1 tablespoon of water or enough to cover the spears. Bring to a boil and simmer for 10–12 minutes, turning the spears over occasionally until they are tender. The cooking time will depend on how thick the stalks are. Set aside in the pan.

Meanwhile, finish the beurre blanc. Set the Champagne reduction in its heatproof bowl over a pot of barely simmering water, being careful not to let the bowl come into contact with the water. Whisk in all the cubes of butter, one by one, until emulsified into a smooth sauce. Season to taste with a little salt and pepper. Remove from the heat but leave the bowl over the hot water to keep warm if you can't serve the dish straightaway, stirring every now and then. The sauce will last for 10 minutes or so like this, but any longer and it might split. Serve the warm sauce spooned over the drained, warm asparagus spears.

Special

Rowley Leigh, chef proprietor of Le Café Anglais in London, is one of the founding fathers of modern British cooking and a successful food writer. His elegant menus make use of French influences and techniques, but remain uncomplicated. Needless to say, this tian is only worth making with good ripe vine or plum tomatoes.

Rowley Leigh's
Tian of tomatoes and eggplants

SERVES 6–8
PREPARATION TIME: 30 MINUTES
COOKING TIME: 35 MINUTES

10½ oz all-butter puff pastry

1½ lb eggplants, sliced ¼ inch thick

¾ cup olive oil

1½ lb ripe tomatoes

4 garlic cloves

1 small bunch flat-leaf parsley, leaves finely chopped

3 tablespoons fresh bread crumbs

Roll out the puff pastry into a disk about 9 inches in diameter and leave to rest on a baking tray.

Brush the eggplant slices well with half the olive oil and cook in a dry frying pan, brushing them with a little more oil if they become dry. They should be golden and cooked through.

Peel the tomatoes by removing the cores and plunging them in boiling water for 10 seconds before refreshing them in plenty of cold water. Slice the tomatoes to the same thickness as the eggplant.

Preheat the oven to 375°F (Gas 5).

Chop the garlic very finely, crushing it with the help of a teaspoon of sea salt. Mix together the garlic, parsley, and bread crumbs to make a persillade.

Arrange the tomatoes and eggplant in overlapping layers on top of the puff pastry, leaving a ⅝ inch border of pastry still showing. Season with a little salt and plenty of freshly ground black pepper before sprinkling the persillade over the top. Spoon the remaining oil over the crumbs and then bake in the oven for about 35 minutes until the pastry is risen and golden. Slide onto a large serving plate and leave to cool.

Making a rotolo undoubtedly involves a bit of love and hard work, but it will repay you handsomely in flavor and compliments. If it makes life easier, you can roast the pumpkin, wilt the spinach, and make the pasta the day before. That way, you'll only have to assemble and simmer the rotolo and make the sage butter on the day.

Pumpkin and spinach rotolo with sage butter

SERVES 6 AS A STARTER
PREPARATION TIME: 45 MINUTES
PLUS CHILLING TIME
COOKING TIME: 1 HOUR

FOR THE PASTA:

2 cups all-purpose flour or Italian type 00 flour, plus extra for rolling out

2 eggs

2 egg yolks

FOR THE FILLING:

a handful of small sage leaves

1 lb peeled pumpkin, cut into ¾ inch cubes

3 tablespoons olive oil

1¼ lb spinach leaves, washed

¼ cup butter

1 heaping cup ricotta, drained

2 tablespoons finely grated Parmesan

a good grating of nutmeg

½ quantity slow-roasted tomatoes (see page 242), made with 3⅓ cups cherry tomatoes

Pulse the pasta ingredients in a food processor until "bread crumbs" form, and tip onto a work surface. Knead for 5 minutes until smooth, soft, and elastic. Form into a disk, wrap in plastic wrap and leave in a cool place for at least 30 minutes.

Preheat the oven to 400°F (Gas 6). Shred a couple of sage leaves finely and toss with the pumpkin and 1 tablespoon olive oil. Season well. Spread on a baking sheet and roast for 30 minutes, or until tender. Wilt the spinach in 1 tablespoon of the butter over medium heat in a large pan. When no water remains, season and set aside to cool, then roughly chop.

Combine the ricotta and Parmesan and season with plenty of nutmeg and salt and pepper. Set aside. Roll the pasta out to form a rectangle 16 x 12 inches, using a small amount of flour to prevent it from sticking. Trim the edges so they are straight and true and lay this rectangle on a clean, flat dishtowel. Wring out any water from the spinach and scatter over the pasta, leaving a border. Dot the spinach with the ricotta and scatter with roasted pumpkin. Roll up from a long edge to form a sausage shape, then roll the dishtowel firmly around it and tie the ends and middle with pieces of string. Lower the rotolo into a large pan of generously salted boiling water and poach gently for 20 minutes. Remove the rotolo from the pan and shake off excess water. Cut the strings.

Heat the remaining 2 tablespoons olive oil in a pan and add the rest of the sage leaves. Cook until crisp, then drain on paper towels. Melt the remaining butter in the pan, and when it starts to turn golden, remove from the heat. Unwrap the rotolo, trim the ends, and slice into 12 pieces. Divide between 6 warmed plates, add a few roasted tomatoes, and spoon the butter over. Finish with crisp sage leaves.

Francesco Mazzei is immensely proud of his Calabrian roots, and this shines through in his bold but refined cooking. The menu at L'Anima, his sleek London restaurant, interprets southern Italian and Moorish dishes, using as much seasonal, local produce as possible. The leafy herb borage grows wild across the Mediterranean, and its mild, cucumber-like flavor makes a beautiful pasta filling.

Francesco Mazzei's
Borage tortelli with sage butter

SERVES 6
PREP TIME: 1 HOUR 10 MINUTES
PLUS RESTING TIME
COOKING TIME: 15 MINUTES

1 quantity rich pasta dough
(see page 251)

FOR THE PASTA FILLING:

2 shallots, finely chopped

¼ cup butter

1½ lb young borage greens

freshly grated nutmeg, to taste

1⅓ cups best-quality ricotta, drained

1¾ oz Parmesan, finely grated,
plus extra to serve

2 teaspoons finely chopped
marjoram leaves

FOR THE SAGE BUTTER:

⅓ cup butter

about 20 small sage leaves

First make your rich pasta dough, and leave it to rest as instructed. You will need to roll it out after you have made your filling.

Gently sweat the shallots in half the butter over low heat until softened but not colored. Blanch the borage in salted, boiling water for a minute or so, drain, and refresh under cold water. Drain well, then chop finely and add to the shallots with a good grating of nutmeg. Stir over the heat for a few minutes, then set aside to cool.

Stir the ricotta, Parmesan, marjoram, and salt and pepper into the borage. Melt the remaining butter and add to the mixture, then set aside to rest and cool while you roll out the pasta as instructed on page 251. Cut the pasta into 3¼ inch squares with a sharp knife. Drop a teaspoon of the borage filling just off-center in each square and brush the edges with water. Fold the dough over to create a triangle, pressing out any air as you go. Holding the triangle with the point at the top, fold the two bottom corners together around your index finger and pinch together firmly to seal, using a little water if needed. Transfer to a sheet of parchment paper to dry a little. Repeat. Drop the tortelli into a large pot of salted, simmering water and cook for 4 minutes or until they rise to the surface. Carefully remove with a slotted spoon.

Meanwhile, heat the butter and sage in a small frying pan until the butter foams and begins to turn a slightly darker brown and the leaves fizz. It should smell nutty, not burnt. The sage leaves should be crisp. Serve the drained tortelli in warmed bowls with the sage butter spooned on top, and grate a little Parmesan over to finish.

Do buy these golden mushrooms whenever you see them, because they are such treasures. Here they are fried in butter with cherries and wine, and spooned over truffle-spiked potato puree with a few truffle pearls to finish. Truffle pearls are an ingenious vegetarian version of caviar made with black truffle and seaweed.

Pan-fried girolles and sour cherries

SERVES 4 AS A MAIN COURSE
PREPARATION TIME: 25 MINUTES
COOKING TIME: 35–40 MINUTES

FOR THE POTATO PURÉE:

2 lb baking potatoes, cut into large chunks

3 tablespoons truffle butter, or 3 tablespoons butter and 2 teaspoons truffle oil

scant ½ cup heavy cream

FOR THE GIROLLES:

1 oz butter

1 tablespoon olive oil

2 garlic cloves, crushed

1¼ lb girolles or golden chanterelles, brushed free of dirt

⅓ cup Madeira or dry sherry

⅓ cup dried sour cherries

⅓ cup vegetable stock (see page 236) or good-quality bought stock

1 tablespoon finely chopped flat-leaf parsley

4 teaspoons truffle pearls, to serve (optional)

Start with the potatoes. Steam them over simmering water for 20–25 minutes until completely tender but not falling apart. Pour all the water out of the saucepan and tip the potatoes into it. Place over low heat for a few minutes, shaking the pan to dry them out.

Press the potatoes through a ricer if you have one—it will produce the smoothest mash—or use a masher to crush them until smooth. Beat in the truffle butter (or butter and truffle oil) and cream, and season generously with salt and pepper. Keep warm.

While the potatoes steam, cook the mushrooms. Melt the butter and oil together in a large frying pan over medium-high heat. Add the garlic and stir, followed by the mushrooms. Toss the pan now and then for a couple of minutes to brown the mushrooms all over. Remove to a plate with a slotted spoon. Pour the Madeira or sherry into the pan and reduce briskly for a minute, then add the cherries and stock and continue to simmer 5 minutes more. Return the mushrooms to the pan. Stir in the parsley and season to taste with salt and pepper.

Serve over the potato puree with a few truffle pearls (if using).

Special

Tom Pemberton, former head chef at St John in London, opened his own restaurant, Hereford Road, in Notting Hill in 2007. He fiercely champions British ingredients such as the Childwickbury goat cheese used here: its fresh and mild flavor shines through in this comforting dish. Wild garlic and morels—spring ingredients—can be replaced with baby spinach and chanterelles in the autumn.

Tom Pemberton's
Pearl barley, mushrooms, and butternut squash

SERVES 4–6
PREPARATION TIME: 25 MINUTES
COOKING TIME: 1 HOUR

¾ oz dried wild mushrooms

8 flat porcini mushrooms

1 small butternut squash or pumpkin, halved, deseeded, and sliced

3 tablespoons olive oil

3 rosemary sprigs

3 thyme sprigs

2 shallots, finely chopped

1 tablespoon butter, for sautéeing

1 cup pearl barley

2 tarragon stalks, roughly chopped

2 bay leaves

3 tablespoons butter, softened

1 garlic clove, crushed

a small handful of fresh morels

a handful of wild garlic leaves

a squeeze of lemon

1⅔ cups Childwickbury cheese, or other fresh goat cheese

Soak the dried mushrooms in ¾ cup plus 1 tablespoon of just-boiled water for 10 minutes. Only the soaking water will be needed in this dish.

Preheat the oven to 400°F (Gas 6). Place the porcini mushrooms and squash or pumpkin in separate trays, drizzle with olive oil, season, and scatter with rosemary and thyme. Roast the mushrooms for 20 minutes and the squash or pumpkin for about 35 minutes.

Gently sauté the shallots in the butter. Rinse the pearl barley in a sieve. Add the rinsed pearl barley, tarragon stalks and bay leaves, the water from the soaked mushrooms, and enough extra water to cover the grains by ¾ inch. Simmer for 25 minutes until the barley is just tender.

Mix the butter with the garlic to make garlic butter. When ready to serve, brown the morels in half the garlic butter and set aside. Slice the roasted mushrooms and add to the pearl barley with the squash or pumpkin and any reserved juices from roasting the vegetables. Reheat together gently with the wild garlic leaves, remaining garlic butter, and a squeeze of lemon, turning through until the leaves just wilt. Remove from the heat and stir in half the cheese and the morels. Serve with the remaining cheese scattered over.

It's a rare recipe that can star as a starter, main, or cheese course. Served as a starter or main, a peppery arugula side salad wouldn't go amiss. As a dessert or cheese course, the tart will stand alone or accompanied by a little crème fraîche. Figs and hard goat cheese also work extremely well instead of the pears and Parmesan.

Pear and Parmesan tarte tatin with thyme pastry

SERVES 6–8
PREPARATION TIME: 20 MINUTES
PLUS CHILLING TIME
COOKING TIME: 40 MINUTES

FOR THE PASTRY:

⅓ cup butter

1⅓ cups all-purpose flour, plus extra for dusting

1 cup Parmesan, finely grated

1 egg, beaten

1 tablespoon thyme leaves

FOR THE REST:

⅓ cup firmly packed, light brown sugar

3 tablespoons butter

3 tablespoons balsamic vinegar

2 tablespoons chopped walnuts

1 tablespoon thyme leaves

6 ripe but firm pears, peeled, quartered, and cored

Start with the pastry. Pulse the butter and flour in a food processor until it resembles fine crumbs. Add a pinch of salt and the cheese and blend for a few seconds. Then add the egg and thyme and blitz again until the pastry just comes together into a ball. Knead briefly until smooth, shape into a disk, and wrap in plastic wrap. Chill for at least 20 minutes.

Preheat the oven to 350°F (Gas 4). In a 10 inch tatin dish or ovenproof frying pan, heat the sugar until it melts, shaking and swirling from time to time so it melts evenly. Increase the heat slightly and add the butter and vinegar, allowing the mixture to bubble for a minute or so. Remove from the heat and sprinkle with the walnuts and thyme. Arrange the pears on top, peeled side down, in a snug, concentric circle.

On a lightly floured surface, roll the rested pastry into a circle ¾ inch larger than your dish or frying pan. Using a rolling pin to pick the pastry up, cover the fruit snugly with it like a blanket, tucking the edges in and under a little to enclose everything securely. Bake for 30 minutes until the pastry is golden and the caramel is bubbling up at the edges. Leave to cool for 10 minutes before placing an inverted plate (ideally one with a lip to catch the sauce) on top of the pan. Wearing oven gloves and holding the plate and pan tightly, flip the whole lot over so that the plate is underneath and the pan is upside down on top of it. Remove the pan to reveal the tart, pushing any dislodged pears back into place if necessary.

Special

This is a decadently rich soufflé cake that will fall and sink slowly as it cools. The middle is dense and mousse-like, the edges crisp, and the salted caramel ribbon swirling through the chocolate gives it an edge over any other torte. It's a good idea to make it a few hours in advance, and serve when cool but not chilled.

Bitter chocolate and salted caramel torte

SERVES 12
PREPARATION TIME: 30 MINUTES
COOKING TIME: ABOUT 40 MINUTES

FOR THE SALTED CARAMEL:

¾ cup turbinado sugar

½ cup heavy cream

½ teaspoon sea salt flakes

½ cup unsalted butter, cubed

FOR THE TORTE:

1⅔ cups dark chocolate (at least 70% cocoa solids), in pieces

scant ⅔ cup unsalted butter, cubed

¾ cup superfine sugar

1 teaspoon vanilla extract

1¼ cups ground almonds

5 medium egg yolks

6 medium egg whites

Line a 10 inch springform cake pan with parchment paper. To make the salted caramel, pour the sugar into a heavy-based pan and add 3 tablespoons of water. Heat gently, stirring only until the sugar dissolves. Turn the heat up to medium-high and allow the syrup to come to a boil undisturbed. Simmer briskly and watch like a hawk until the caramel turns a rich amber color. Swirl the pan to prevent "hot spots" but don't stir or the caramel will crystallize. Remove the pan from the heat and stir in the cream and salt; it's sure to hiss and splutter. Now stir in the butter cubes until a smooth caramel forms, and set aside to cool.

Preheat the oven to 350°F (Gas 4). To make the torte, melt the chocolate, butter, and sugar together in a heatproof bowl set over simmering water. (You can melt everything in a saucepan set over very low heat if you prefer, but go gently in case it burns.) Remove from the heat and stir until smooth, then mix in the vanilla and almonds, followed by the egg yolks, one by one.

Whisk the egg whites in a clean bowl until they hold stiff peaks. Using a metal spoon, fold 1 large tablespoon of the egg whites into the chocolate mixture to loosen it, then fold in the rest, being careful to retain as much air as possible. Scrape into the cake pan and smooth the top. Pour or spoon the caramel over the top in a big circular swirl, moving from the center out. Use a skewer or sharp knife to mix the caramel a little deeper into the batter, but don't overdo it. Bake for about 30 minutes until puffed up but still wobbly in the center. Cool completely in the pan before slicing and serving with cream or ice cream.

Special

If an almond tart isn't deep and buttery with a burnished shell, it isn't worth the effort or the calories. There will be no disappointments here with this divine tart, which delivers on every count.

Rich almond tart with red berry compote

SERVES 10–12
PREPARATION TIME: 40 MINUTES
PLUS CHILLING TIME
COOKING TIME: 1 HOUR 20 MINUTES

FOR THE PASTRY:

1½ cups all-purpose flour, plus a little extra for dusting

½ cup butter, diced

½ teaspoon salt

½ cup confectioners' sugar

1 egg yolk

2–4 teaspoons iced water

FOR THE ALMOND FILLING:

1½ cups blanched almonds

2 tablespoons all-purpose flour

1 cup unsalted butter

1¼ cups superfine sugar

1 vanilla pod, split and seeds scraped out

4 eggs

2⅓ cups seasonal berries, such as blueberries, raspberries, blackberries, red currants, or black currants

FOR THE COMPOTE:

2⅓ cups seasonal berries, as above

3 tablespoons superfine sugar

1 tablespoon balsamic vinegar

chilled crème fraîche, to serve

Preheat the oven to 325°F (Gas 3). To make the pastry, pulse the flour, butter, salt, and sugar in a food processor until the mixture looks like fine bread crumbs. Add the egg yolk and 2 teaspoons of the iced water, then pulse just enough to bring it all together into a dough. You may need another teaspoon or two of iced water, but don't add too much or the pastry will get sticky. Knead very briefly until smooth, form into a disk, and wrap in plastic wrap. Chill for at least 30 minutes. Roll out the pastry on a lightly floured surface until it forms a large enough circle to line a deep 10 inch pie pan that has a removable base. You shouldn't need to butter the pan first. Press the pastry right into the pan and use a sharp knife to trim off any overhanging excess. Chill for at least 30 minutes.

Meanwhile, use a food processor to grind the almonds and flour together finely. The flour should stop the almonds from turning oily. Tip into a bowl. Now add to the food processor the butter, all but 4 tablespoons of the sugar, and vanilla seeds (save the pod) and mix until light and fluffy. Add the eggs, one by one, with the motor still running, until completely blended. Scrape into the bowl with the almonds and mix well. Scatter the berries across the base of the pastry and spoon the almond filling over the fruit. Smooth the top and sprinkle evenly with the remaining sugar. Bake for about 1 hour 20 minutes until golden and risen.

Meanwhile, make the compote. Gently heat the berries with the empty vanilla pod, sugar, and vinegar until the fruit just starts to bleed its juice. Remove from the heat. Cool the tart before serving with the berry compote and crème fraîche.

Special

I find it much more effective to make smaller quantities of really special preserves than endless pots of everyday jams that sit sullenly at the back of the cupboard for months. This black fig jam is intensely rich, and it's the perfect foil for cheeses, crisp crackers, or perhaps little blue cheese tarts still warm from the oven.

Black fig jam for cheese and canapés

MAKES 2 JARS
PREPARATION TIME: 5 MINUTES
PLUS MACERATING TIME
COOKING TIME: 40 MINUTES

1 lb 12 oz ripe black figs, halved

½ teaspoon fennel seeds

1⅓ cups turbinado sugar

juice of 1 lemon

Stir the figs, fennel seeds, and sugar together in a bowl. Cover and set aside for 4 hours or chill overnight.

Tip the fig mixture into a large saucepan and slowly heat through. Once the mixture has come to a boil, scoop out the figs with a slotted spoon and reserve in a bowl. Turn up the heat and simmer the syrup briskly until it reaches the "hard ball" stage at around 235°F (Gas ½). If you don't have a thermometer, scoop a tiny amount of syrup out with a teaspoon and drop into a cup of cold water; it should form a hard ball if ready.

Return the figs to the syrup and continue to simmer for about 25 minutes until thickened, stirring occasionally to break the fruit up. Stir in the lemon juice.

Place in sterilized jars and keep in a cool, dark place.

Special

Basics

Chapter Nine

These delicious butters are more suggestions than rigid recipes, and have many variations. Group complementary ingredients together and experiment, but start with the ideas below. The butters can be tossed with simple steamed vegetables, cooked pasta, whole grains, and more. You can even freeze them so you have them on standby.

Flavored butters

MAKES 9 OZ PER VARIETY
PREPARATION TIME: 15 MINUTES
PLUS CHILLING TIME

flavorings (see method)

1 cup unsalted butter, softened

1 teaspoon sea salt

Beat your choice of flavorings below into the softened butter with the salt. Spoon onto a sheet of greaseproof paper and roll into a cylinder, twisting the ends to close. Chill for at least an hour to firm up so that you can slice circles off when needed. The wrapped and chilled butters will keep for at least 4 weeks. If you choose to freeze the butter, slice into disks before wrapping the cylinder. Keep the frozen butter for up to 3 months, snapping off a disk or two as needed.

Lime and chili butter

Finely grated zest of 2 limes; 2 red chilies, deseeded and finely chopped.

Blue cheese and black pepper butter

⅔ cup Roquefort, finely crumbled; 1 teaspoon thyme leaves; 2 teaspoons crushed black peppercorns.

Garlic-herb butter

2 fat garlic cloves, crushed; 3 tablespoons finely chopped basil leaves or chives; 2 tablespoons pine nuts, toasted and chopped.

Parsley butter

3 tablespoons finely chopped parsley; ½ garlic clove, crushed; ½ teaspoon crushed black peppercorns.

Mayonnaise

2 egg yolks
1 teaspoon Dijon mustard
1 cup plus 1 tablespoon very mild olive oil
a good squeeze of lemon

Blend or beat the egg yolks with a generous
seasoning of salt and pepper and the mustard.
As you blend or beat, start to add the olive oil,
drop by slow drop. Tentatively increase the
drops to a thin trickle as you continue to blend.
Add about half the oil, then beat in the lemon
juice. Continue adding the oil as before until
it has all gone and the mayonnaise is thick
and glossy. Taste and add a touch more salt,
pepper, or lemon juice if needed. To make herb
mayonnaise, stir in 2 tablespoons chopped
fresh herbs at the end. To make aïoli, add
2–3 fat, crushed garlic cloves with the egg
yolks. To make red pepper aïoli, stir 2 roughly
puréed roasted red peppers (from a jar is fine)
into the finished aïoli. Makes 1 cup.

Gomashio

3 tablespoons sea salt
1½ cups sesame seeds

Toast the salt in a dry frying pan, stirring often,
until it turns gray. Tip into a mortar and pestle,
spice grinder, or food processor. Toast the
sesame seeds in the same pan until they smell
fragrant. Grind the salt and seeds together, by
hand or by machine, until broken down but not
too smooth, or the mixture will become oily.
Store in a tightly sealed jar and use within
2 months. Makes 1 large jar.

Balsamic vinaigrette

2 tablespoons balsamic vinegar
a pinch of superfine sugar
4 tablespoons extra virgin olive oil
1 teaspoon Dijon mustard
1 tablespoon chopped basil

This dressing is especially good with tomatoes
and roasted Mediterranean vegetables. For
variation, you could also add a whisper of
garlic before blending. Place all the ingredients
in a mini food processor with 1 tablespoon
water and pulse until blended. Makes
about ½ cup.

Vegetable stock

1 tablespoon sunflower oil
2 large onions, sliced
2 large carrots, sliced
10 celery stalks, sliced
6 garlic cloves, bruised
4 chard stalks, sliced
¼ cup brown lentils
3 bay leaves
a small bunch of parsley stalks
1 teaspoon black peppercorns
1 teaspoon sea salt

Heat the oil in a large saucepan. Slowly brown
the onions and carrots, stirring, for about
20 minutes. The vegetables should be golden
and caramelized. Add the remaining ingredients
with 8½ cups cold water, bring to a simmer and
bubble gently for 1 hour. Strain and discard the
vegetables. Return the stock to the pan on the
heat and reduce to the desired strength. Makes
about 2 quarts.

Horseradish dressing

2 tablespoons crème fraîche
4 tablespoons walnut oil
1 tablespoon finely grated horseradish, or more to taste
juice of 1 lemon
a pinch of superfine sugar

This is strictly for robustly flavored vegetables and leaves, as it takes a certain strength to stand up to peppery horseradish. Whisk all the ingredients together with 2 tablespoons cold water to loosen. Season to taste with salt and pepper. Makes ½ cup.

Salsa verde dressing

1 small bunch parsley, chopped
½ small bunch mint, chopped
¼ cup extra virgin olive oil, plus extra if needed
1 fat garlic clove, crushed
2 tablespoons capers, rinsed, drained, and chopped
1½ tablespoons Dijon mustard
2 tablespoons red wine vinegar

In a small bowl, cover the chopped herbs with olive oil—start with ¼ cup and see how you go. Stir in the remaining ingredients and season with salt and pepper to taste. The sauce should have a spoonable consistency, so add more olive oil if needed. Makes about 1 cup.

Pesto

1 fat garlic clove, roughly chopped
a pinch of sea salt
a large handful of basil leaves
⅓ cup pine nuts
½ cup extra virgin olive oil
⅔ cup Parmesan, finely grated

In a food processor pulse together the garlic, salt, basil leaves, and pine nuts, scraping down the sides now and then. Add the cheese and trickle in the oil until blended. To make parsley, peppery arugula, or watercress pesto, replace the basil with your herb of choice and swap the pine nuts with roughly chopped, blanched almonds. To make sun-dried tomato pesto, simply add 5 drained and chopped sun-dried tomato halves when pounding or blending the basil. To make vegan pesto, omit the cheese and increase the quantity of pine nuts or almonds to 3 tablespoons. Makes 1 jar.

Sweet lemon dressing

½ garlic clove, crushed
1 tablespoon mild honey
1 teaspoon whole-grain mustard
finely grated zest and juice of 1 lemon
⅓ cup olive oil

Robust leaves—endive, radicchio, arugula, and watercress—all bring out the best in this dressing. If you'd rather use a milder leaf, you might want to replace the honey with 2 tablespoons finely grated Parmesan to pep it up and balance out the flavors. Combine all the ingredients in a screw-top jar with salt and pepper, and shake until thoroughly blended. Makes about ½ cup.

Sauces

Fig tapenade

Place ½ cup ready-to-eat, chopped dried figs in a pan with ½ cup water and simmer for 15 minutes, stirring, until tender. Remove from the heat and cool. Use a mortar and pestle or food processor to crush ½ garlic clove, 1 cup pitted Kalamata olives, 2 tablespoons rinsed and drained capers, the figs and their liquid, a twist of black pepper, and 2 tablespoons thyme leaves. Pulse and loosen with extra virgin olive oil.

Blender hollandaise

Melt ½ cup butter in a small pan. Blend 2 egg yolks in a small blender with 2 tablespoons boiling water and season with a pinch of salt and a little black pepper. With the motor on, very gradually trickle in the hot butter until a thick sauce forms. Add a couple of tablespoons of lemon juice and blend again. Check the lemon and seasoning before serving.

Gorgonzola

Soften 2 finely chopped shallots in a little butter until translucent. Add 1⅓ cups chopped Gorgonzola (or Roquefort if you prefer) and stir gently until the cheese melts. Stir in ½ cup of heavy cream and mix well. Season with black pepper. A little finely chopped parsley stirred in at the end makes a nice addition. Delicious stirred through pasta.

Take Six

4

Walnut tarator

This Turkish sauce is a bit like a nut pesto. It is wonderful with roasted or grilled vegetables or in flatbread wraps. Pulse 1⅔ cups shelled walnuts in a food processor with a fat, crushed garlic clove and a good pinch of salt until quite finely ground. Gradually pour in 2 tablespoons red wine vinegar, ½ cup water, and ¼ cup extra virgin olive oil as you process again to form a creamy but not completely smooth sauce.

6

Best tomato

Peel and halve a small onion and lightly bash a whole, peeled garlic clove. Place in a saucepan with two 14 oz cans of best-quality plum tomatoes and ¼ cup butter (or ¼ cup extra virgin olive oil if you prefer). Place over a very gentle heat and slowly simmer, stirring occasionally, for about 40–50 minutes. Season with salt and pepper and discard the onion before using. The garlic will have melted away.

5

Béchamel

In a saucepan bring to a boil: 4 cups whole milk; 1 small, peeled and halved onion; 10 black peppercorns; and 2 bay leaves. Remove from the heat and infuse for 20 minutes or so. Melt ¼ cup butter in a pan and add ⅓ cup all-purpose flour, stirring until a smooth paste forms. Cook gently for a minute or so, stirring, then gradually add the infused milk, tentatively at first, beating all the while. Use a whisk at this stage to prevent lumps. When the milk has been incorporated, bring the sauce to a boil and simmer gently for a couple of minutes. Season and add a generous grating of nutmeg. Cover to prevent a skin forming and set aside to cool.

Chili tomato jam

10 mild red chilies, deseeded
2 shallots, roughly chopped
1½ inch piece ginger, roughly chopped
2 lemongrass stalks, roughly chopped
1⅓ cups cherry tomatoes, halved
¼ cup firmly packed palm sugar or light brown sugar
4 tablespoons rice wine vinegar
2 tablespoons soy sauce

Place the chilies in a food processor with the shallots, ginger, and lemongrass. Pulse, scraping down the sides every few seconds, until finely chopped. Scrape into a saucepan with the tomatoes and sugar, and cook over medium-high heat for about 20 minutes. Stir often until the liquid evaporates and the sugar caramelizes. Now add the vinegar and soy sauce and simmer until the liquid evaporates. Season with salt to taste. Spoon into a sterilized jar, cover, and keep chilled for up to 4 weeks. Makes 1 large jar.

Rustic, slow-roasted tomato sauce

1½ cups slow-roasted tomatoes (see recipe this page)
2 cups jar tomato puree
a small handful of basil leaves
2 tablespoons extra virgin olive oil

This is a deep and intense sauce that can be made almost instantly if you have a batch of slow-roasted tomatoes on hand. Add chopped red chili or crushed garlic before blending to ring the changes. Simply blend all the ingredients together in a food processor or blender until almost smooth. Makes about 3½ cups.

Slow-roasted tomatoes

2¼ lb ripe, sweet tomatoes, halved
2 tablespoons superfine sugar
2 tablespoons chopped fresh rosemary leaves
3 garlic cloves, finely chopped

Preheat the oven to 225ºF (Gas ½). Lay the tomatoes out on 2 baking sheets, cut sides up. Sprinkle with salt and pepper, sugar, rosemary, and garlic, and drizzle with olive oil. Roast for about 4 hours—depending on the size or variety of tomato—until shrunken and a little blackened at the edges. If your tomatoes are very large, they can take up to 6 hours, but if you use cherry tomatoes, they will take about 3 hours.

Pepper compote

3 red peppers
3 long red chilies
1 red onion, halved and finely sliced
2 tablespoons olive oil
1 garlic clove, crushed
1 tablespoon light brown sugar
3 tablespoons sherry vinegar
a pinch of sweet smoked paprika

Blacken the peppers and chilies over a gas flame or under a very hot broiler, turning with tongs every minute or so until charred all over. Remove to a bowl, cover with plastic wrap, and set aside for a few minutes. Scrape the skin from peppers and chilies, halve them, and scrape out the seeds. Chop the flesh roughly. Gently fry the onion in the oil until softened, then reduce the heat and add the garlic and chopped peppers. Cook for 5 minutes more, add the sugar, vinegar, and paprika, and cook until caramelized. Spoon into a sterilized jar or dish and keep chilled. Makes 1 jar.

Satay sauce

1 garlic clove, chopped
2 shallots, roughly chopped
1–2 red chilies, roughly chopped
1 tablespoon peanut oil
2 teaspoons superfine sugar
1 cup peanuts, toasted and roughly chopped
1 tablespoon soy sauce
1¾ cups coconut milk
juice of 1 lime

Gently fry the garlic, shallots, and red chilies in the oil until soft but not colored. Add the sugar and peanuts and cook for a further 2 minutes until caramelized. Now stir in the soy and coconut milk and simmer for 5 minutes. Keep the texture chunky, or blend briefly in a food processor. Add the lime juice and season with a little extra soy if needed. Satay sauce will keep in the refrigerator for 2 weeks or more. Makes about 2 cups.

Charmoula dressing

1 small bunch cilantro
1 small bunch parsley
1 tablespoon cumin seeds, toasted
finely grated zest and juice of 1 lemon
¼ cup extra virgin olive oil
½ teaspoon salt
1 garlic clove, crushed
½ teaspoon paprika
1 teaspoon ras el hanout

Place all the ingredients in a food processor and pulse until finely chopped. Add a little more olive oil if it seems too thick, and season with black pepper. Keep covered in the refrigerator for up to 2 weeks, ready to use whenever the mood takes you. Makes 1 jar.

Ginger and lime dipping sauce

¼ cup boiling water
1½ tablespoons superfine sugar
2 tablespoons vegetarian fish sauce or soy sauce
2 tablespoons rice wine vinegar
juice of ½ lime
1½ inch piece ginger, finely chopped
1 fat garlic clove, finely chopped
1 red chili, deseeded and finely chopped (optional)

Pour the boiling water over the sugar and stir to dissolve. Add all the remaining ingredients —leaving out the chili if you like—and mix well. Leave to stand for a few minutes before using. Makes ½ cup.

Pickled fruit for cheese and salads

2 cups red wine vinegar
2 tablespoons superfine sugar
1 tablespoon sea salt
1 tablespoon black peppercorns
3 rosemary sprigs
1 lb fresh fruit, trimmed, pitted, sliced, or halved, as appropriate

Place all the ingredients except the fruit in a large saucepan, add ⅔ cup water, and bring to a boil. Add the fruit. Divide between sterilized jars and seal. Keep in a cool, dark place for at least 2 weeks before opening—a month if you can. To serve, simply remove as much fruit as you need from the jar with a slotted spoon. The leftover pickling liquid can be strained and used in salad dressings. Once opened, the pickles will last for at least 4 weeks, but keep refrigerated. Makes 3 jars.

Menu Ideas

Winter dinner

Blood orange, mozzarella, toasted
sourdough, and radicchio salad (page 82)

Parsnip, sage, and
mascarpone risotto (page 172)

Rich almond tart with
red berry compote (page 228)

Black fig jam, with cheese
and crackers (page 230)

Spring brunch

Mango and cashew smoothies (page 32)

Toasted honey and pumpkin seed
granola with yogurt, served
with rhubarb compote (page 34)

Baked ricotta with avocado (page 24)

Pizza Bianca (page 136)

Salad potato griddle cakes with olives
and poached eggs (page 160)

Sunday lunch

Butter bean and celery root velouté
with charmoula (page 126)

Pearl barley, mushrooms and
butternut squash (page 222)

Greens dressed with
walnut tarator (page 186)

Pear and Parmesan tarte tatin
with thyme pastry (page 224)

Fast dinner
for friends

Shopska salad (page 168)

Fennel and lemon risotto (page 201)

Asparagus with broche crumbs (page 186)

Warm salted caramel sauce with bought
vanilla ice cream
(make the salted caramel from the bitter chocolate
and salted caramel torte recipe on page 226)

Menu Ideas

Romantic dinner

White gazpacho (page 116)

Pumpkin and spinach rotolo with
sage butter (as a main course, page 216)

Bitter chocolate and
salted caramel torte (page 226)

Pickled fruit to serve with a
cheese platter (page 244)

Southeast Asian lunch

Summer spring rolls (page 206)

Crispy five-spice tofu with
soy dipping sauce (page 154)

Braised baby eggplant with bok choy,
peanuts, and Thai basil, served with
steamed rice (page 182)

Ripe melon, papaya, and
mango slices, to finish

Summer picnic

Gazpacho Andaluz (page 114)

Pissaladière (page 194)

Nectarine and tomato salad with buffalo
mozzarella (page 210)

No-knead sourdough loaf (page 134)

Summer berries with home-made yogurt
(instructions for yogurt page 36)

Drinks party

Roasted, spiced chickpeas (page 105)

Robust caponata spooned
onto panelle (page 46)

Betel leaf wraps with coconut
and cashews (page 208)

Puy lentil hummus, carrot and cumin
hummus, garlic toasts (page 54)

Chervil pancakes with eggplant caviar
and pomegranate (page 204)

Glossary

Betel leaves

The edible leaves of the Piper betle plant are used extensively throughout Southeast Asia. When used as a wrap for food, keep the glossy side of each heart-shaped leaf on the outside. Look for them in the chilled fresh vegetable section of Southeast Asian food shops. Keep refrigerated and use within a few days of purchase.

Blind baking

Pastry tart shells often need to be cooked before filling to ensure they are crisp and not soggy underneath. To do this, line a pie plate with raw pastry and chill. Cover with parchment paper and heap pie weights, dried beans, or uncooked rice into the tart cavity, then bake at 375°F (Gas 5) for 15 minutes. Remove the beans and foil or paper, and return the pastry to the oven for a further 5–10 minutes until it looks dry and "sandy" but still pale.

Burrata

This decadently rich buffalo or cow's-milk cheese from southern Italy is similar to mozzarella, but each sphere of cheese contains an indulgent center of cream. The trick is to eat it as fresh as possible to enjoy the best of its mild, buttery flavor. You can order it from good Italian delis.

Buttermilk

Traditionally, buttermilk was a watery by-product of butter making, but these days is made by souring skimmed milk to produce a dairy product similar to thin yogurt. Buttermilk produces tender pancakes and light, quick breads when combined with baking soda.

Chinese black vinegar

This sweetly complex vinegar is made from glutinous rice and malt. Use in small amounts in dipping sauces, marinades, stir-fries, and braises. Rice vinegar with a pinch of brown sugar added is a good alternative.

Chipotle pepper

Jalepeño peppers are smoke-dried in Mexico to make the fiery and complex chipotle. They are available dried, or in a paste in jars, and will add smoky heat to your cooking. Add a whole pepper to simmering stews or soups, or a teaspoonful or two of the paste. Go carefully, as the heat is intense.

Daikon, mooli, or white radish

This large carrot-shaped radish is crisp, white, and very popular throughout Asia. Because of its size and mild flavor, it is often sliced or shredded and then pickled, to be eaten as a condiment or in stir-fries. You'll find daikon in specialty food shops or large supermarkets. Store in the fridge or a cool pantry.

Dry roasting and oven toasting

Spices, nuts, and seeds often benefit from being gently toasted in a completely dry frying pan over medium heat before grinding or using in a recipe. This will bring out the fragrance and make nuts taste nuttier by coaxing out their oils. To toast nuts and seeds in the oven, spread out on a baking tray and bake at 300°F (Gas 2) for 8–10 minutes (keep an eye on them!), shaking the tray once or twice to redistribute to ensure they toast evenly.

Gram flour

Also known as chickpea flour or besan, gram flour is made from chickpeas. Gluten-free, it has a toasty, slightly nutty taste and is fantastic in batters and can hold vegetables together in bhajis or pakoras. It is famously used in socca, the traditional Niçoise fritters, and the similar Italian farinata and panelle.

Harissa

Based on red chilies and hot paprika, this oily North African paste often contains other spices and aromatics like cumin, coriander, garlic, lemons, pimiento, and even rosebuds. Buy from specialty shops or supermarkets and refrigerate once opened. Add to marinades and dressings, tagines, soups, and dips.

Lemongrass

To use this mellow, lemony grass in curry pastes, dressings, stir-fries, and sauces, trim the hard base from the roots, snip about an inch off the top, then peel away the outer layers to reveal the softer, purplish core. Chop this soft middle into rings or fine dice, discarding any hard stalk. Bash the stalk with a rolling pin and add to rice, or to sauces as they simmer. Lemongrass combines successfully with sugar in sweet dishes.

Pomegranate molasses

This sweet-and-sour, dark red syrup is made by boiling pomegranate juice down until it is thick and sticky. Its tart flavor is used in many Middle Eastern dishes, most commonly to enhance meat and poultry, but is also wonderful added to dressings for roasted vegetables. Lemon juice mixed with honey, or tamarind, can be used as a substitute. It can also be diluted to make a drink.

Pomelo

This large, green or yellow citrus fruit is native to Southeast Asia. Its pale yellow or pink flesh (depending on the variety) will separate easily into segments if you pry off the thick layer of white pith and membranes. To do this, score the fruit into sections from top to bottom and peel away the skin and as much white pith as possible, then pull the fruit in half.

Ras el hanout

Ras el hanout translates literally as "top of the shop" in Arabic; it's a fragrant Moroccan spice mix blended from the best of the spice merchant's shop. Some versions contain over one hundred different ingredients, but it commonly includes coriander, cumin, cinnamon, turmeric, clove, nutmeg, cardamom, and chilies. Use in marinades, dressings, and sauces.

Rice wine vinegar

This vinegar made from fermented rice is commonly used in Southeast Asian cooking and is pale, clear, and sharp—ideal for dipping sauces, pickles, and marinades. It is widely available in supermarkets and specialty food shops.

Rich pasta dough

Make this delicious pasta dough for Francesco Mazzei's borage tortelli with sage butter recipe on page 218, or your own pasta dishes.

INGREDIENTS

2 cups all-purpose or Italian type 00 flour, plus more as needed
9 egg yolks
semolina flour, for dusting

Pour the flour onto a clean work surface and make a well in the center like a volcano well. Tip the egg yolks into the well. Using one hand, mix the yolks into the flour gradually, using a circular motion to incorporate more and more flour as you go. Stop when enough flour has been mixed in to make a slightly flaky ball. You may not need all the flour, or you may need a little more. Wash and dry your hands, then knead the dough for about 10 minutes until very smooth and silken. Add extra flour as needed to stop it sticking. Wrap in plastic wrap and leave to rest for at least 30 minutes or up to 1 hour. You can make the dough a day ahead and chill, well wrapped.

When you have made the filling, cut the dough into 6 even pieces (cover the unused dough to stop it drying out). Run each piece through a pasta machine on its widest setting. Do this several times, folding the dough over on itself twice before you pass it through the machine again. Dust with semolina to stop it sticking. Don't be alarmed if the dough looks a bit lacy at one point—it will work out in the end if you fold it and pass it through the machine a few more times. Now, stop folding the pasta over and just pass it through the rollers, reducing the setting one notch each time. When you reach the thinnest setting but one, lay the rolled sheet of dough out on a work surface dusted with semolina. If you don't own a pasta machine, roll the pasta out by hand on a lightly floured surface until very thin. Continue with the borage tortelli and sage butter recipe as instructed, or whatever recipe you are are using.

Sambal oelek

This vibrant Indonesian chili paste is used to pep up curries, marinades, and dipping sauces. Add it sparingly, because its red chili content can pack quite a punch. Substitute with finely chopped red chili, ground with a little salt, if you can't find it.

Seasoning

The finest sea salt flakes and freshly crushed black peppercorns really will make a difference to your cooking, and you will probably need to add less than if you use generic table salt and sneeze-worthy preground pepper. Keep tasting your food and adjusting the seasoning accordingly. If you add a touch too much salt by mistake, a squeeze of lemon juice or a spoonful of vinegar can remedy the situation.

Soy sauce

This thin, salty Southeast Asian sauce is made from fermented soy beans, wheat, yeast, salt, and sugar. It is available in light or dark: dark soy is slightly thicker and sweeter than light. If you are avoiding wheat, seek out the wheat-free equivalent, tamari.

Sterilizing

To sterilize jars and lids for preserves and pickles, wash in hot, soapy water, then carefully rinse again with freshly boiled water. Preheat the oven to 300°F (Gas 2) and dry the jars and lids on a tray in the oven for 10 minutes. Fill them with the hot preserve or pickle while still warm to prevent cracking, and seal immediately by screwing the lids on tightly.

Tahini

This sesame seed paste is used in one form or another throughout the Middle East and Asia. The variety used in this book, and most commonly found in our markets, is light tahini paste, so called because the sesame seeds have been hulled before roasting and grinding. This process takes away much of the bitterness found in rustic versions. The putty-colored paste should be chilled after opening. Use it make hummus, dressings, and sauces.

Tamarind

The sticky seed pod from the tamarind tree is commonly used in Southeast Asian and Indian dishes to add an appealing honeyed sourness. The brown pods house hard seeds that are embedded in a dense sweet-and-sour pulp. Convenient tamarind purée can be purchased in jars, but the blocks of fresh tamarind pulp have a better flavor. If using a block of pulp place ¼ cup of it in a bowl and cover with ⅔ cup boiling water. Leave to soften for a few minutes, then stir well and strain to remove the fibers and seeds. Use as you would the bought purée

Tempeh

Made from fermented or cultured soy beans, tempeh is a pressed, pale cake with a firm texture that is rich in protein, fiber and vitamins. It can be sliced, cubed, or even grated to be grilled, stir-fried, or added to vegetable patties or curries. Tempeh responds well to brining or marinating with aromatics and spices, and is readily available from health food shops.

Toasted sesame oil

This amber-hued oil is pressed from roasted or toasted sesame seeds. This process lends the oil a dark caramel color and the aromatic flavor essential to many Chinese, Korean, and some Southeast Asian dishes. Add a few drops at the end of cooking so the heat does not destroy the oil's flavor and use sparingly or its nutty tones may be overwhelming.

Vegetarian "fish sauce"

You may have to search hard for this ingredient, but it does exist! Good Southeast Asian shops should stock bottles of this salty, mushroom-based alternative to a true fish sauce. If you can't find t, substitute with light soy sauce.

Index

A

almonds: almond milk and maple
  oatmeal 22
  apricot and almond granola 34
  bitter chocolate and salted caramel
    torte 226
  charred baby cauliflower 150
  rich almond tart with red berry
    compote 228
  warm salad of slow-roasted tomatoes,
    labne, and almonds 76
  white gazpacho 116
artichokes: artichoke, orzo, and fava bean
    salad 86
  artichokes with lemon and oregano
    bread crumbs 192
  artichokes, Jerusalem: see
    Jerusalem artichokes
asparagus: asparagus with brioche
    crumbs 186
  grilled asparagus and warm pearl barley
    salad 96
  white asparagus with Champagne beurre
    blanc 212
avocados: baked ricotta with avocado 24
  cumin potato skins and guacamole
    salsa 56
  guacamole salad 90
  raw vegetable and avocado soup 108
  salad of avocado with white radish and
    carrot pickle 84
  sprouted chickpea and avocado
    hummus 60

B

balsamic vinaigrette 236
barley: see pearl barley
basil: basil oil 210
  pesto 238
bean sprouts: mushroom banh khoai 58
  Vietnamese hot and sour soup 110
beans 16
  sprouts 92–3
béchamel sauce 241
beets: beet and fig carpaccio 187
  beet and porcini broth 124
  shaved salad with toasted seeds 74
betel leaf wraps with coconut and
    cashews 208
black beans: smoky black bean and roasted
    tomato soup 118
black fig jam 230
blackberry milkshake 32
blood orange, mozzarella, toasted
    sourdough, and radicchio salad 82
blue cheese and black pepper butter 234
bok choy, braised baby eggplant with 182
borage tortelli with sage butter 218
bread 128–39
  baked ricotta with avocado 24

blood orange, mozzarella, toasted
    sourdough, and radicchio salad 82
  cauliflower pangrattato 201
  grilled Caesar salad 102
  no-knead sourdough loaf 134
  olive stromboli 132
  panzanella burrata 168
  parsnip and rosemary rolls 138
  pizza bianca 136
  quick soda bread 130
  roasted garlic toasts 54
  toasted garlic bread crumbs 104
  toasted goat cheese and charred tomato
    panini 30
  white gazpacho 116
broccoli: orecchiette pasta with broccoli and
    pine nuts 158
  spring vegetable pakoras 66
bulgur wheat: green tabbouleh 94
butter bean and celery root velouté 126
butternut squash: butternut squash falafel
    42
  pearl barley, mushrooms, and butternut
    squash 222
  shredded root vegetable gratin 190
  winter squash and corn chowder 122
butters, flavored 234

C

cabbage: potsticker dumplings 44
Caesar salad 102
Camembert, watercress, and marinated
    figs 100
caponata on panelle 46
caramel: bitter chocolate and salted caramel
    torte 226
carrots: carrot fritters 146
  carrot hummus 54
  raw vegetable and avocado soup 108
  salad of avocado with white radish and
    carrot pickle 84
  a winter salad 78
cashews: betel leaf wraps with coconut
    and cashews 208
  cashew fried rice 162
  mango and cashew smoothie 32
cauliflower: cauliflower pangrattato 201
  charred baby cauliflower 150
celery root: butter bean and celery root velouté
    126
  celery root rémoulade 152
  soft-boiled duck egg with celery root
    dipping chips 164
Champagne beurre blanc 212
chana chaat 98
chard and brie mini muffins 40
charmoula dressing 244
  butter bean and celery root velouté
    with 126
  giant couscous salad with 80

cheese 19
  artichoke, orzo, and fava bean salad
    with shaved pecorino 86
  baked ricotta with avocado 24
  blood orange, mozzarella, toasted
    sourdough, and radicchio salad 82
  blue cheese and black pepper
    butter 234
  borage tortelli with sage butter 218
  Camembert, watercress, and marinated
    figs 100
  carrot fritters with halloumi 146
  chard and brie mini muffins 40
  crisp Parmesan lace 105
  fine white lasagne with many layers 196
  Gorgonzola sauce 240
  grilled Caesar salad 102
  grilled vegetable pizza 174
  labne 50–1
  nectarine and tomato salad with buffalo
    mozzarella 210
  olive stromboli 132
  oven-baked pea, barley, and fava bean
    frittata 198
  parsnip, sage, and mascarpone risotto
    172
  pear and Parmesan tarte tatin 224
  pesto 238
  pressed leek terrine 68
  pumpkin and spinach rotolo 216
  ricotta gnocchi gratin 176
  shredded root vegetable gratin with
    crème fraîche and Gruyère 190
  spiced pumpkin and feta puff pastry
    tarts 64
  spinach, herb, and ricotta crêpes
    gratin 188
  sunblush terrine 62
  warm salad of slow-roasted tomatoes,
    labne, and almonds 76
  zucchini and Taleggio risotto 200
  see also goat cheese
cherries: cherry and coconut granola 34
  pan-fried girolles and sour cherries 220
cherry tomato tarte tatin 169
chervil pancakes 204
chestnuts with Jerusalem artichokes 180
chickpeas: butternut squash falafel 42
  carrot hummus 54
  chana chaat 98
  roasted, spiced chickpeas 105
  sprouted chickpea and avocado
    hummus 60
chilies: chili and crushed walnut rigatoni 166
  chili tomato jam 242
  lime and chili butter 234
  pepper compote 242
  salsa 118
  satay sauce 244
  tomato and spinach dhal 169

chocolate: bitter chocolate and salted caramel torte 226
chocolate and fig granola 34
chowder, winter squash and corn 122
cilantro: butternut squash falafel 42
carrot fritters 146
charmoula dressing 244
coconut: betel leaf wraps with coconut and cashews 208
cherry and coconut granola 34
coconut milk: satay sauce 244
corn: salsa 118
winter squash and corn chowder 122
couscous: baked red onions stuffed with toasted, spiced couscous 178
giant couscous salad 80
cranberries, quinoa with parsley pesto and 88
crêpes: spinach, herb, and ricotta crêpes gratin 188
cucumber: chilled cucumber and lovage soup 112
cucumber yogurt 42
gazpacho Andaluz 114
cumin potato skins 56
curry: sambal telur 184

D
dairy products 19
dhal, tomato and spinach 169
Dijon mayonnaise 68
duck egg with celery root dipping chips 164
dumplings, potsticker 44

E
eggplant: braised baby eggplant with bok choy, peanuts, and Thai basil 182
chervil pancakes with eggplant caviar and pomegranate 204
Japanese eggplant with miso 148
robust caponata spooned onto panelle 46
tian of tomatoes and eggplant 214
eggs 19
oven-baked pea, barley, and fava bean frittata 198
salad potato griddle cakes with olives and poached eggs 160
sambal telur 184
soft-boiled duck egg with celery root dipping chips 164
squash blossom and tomato frittatas 52

F
falafel, butternut squash 42
faro: a winter salad 78
fava beans: artichoke, orzo, and fava bean salad 86
oven-baked pea, barley, and fava bean frittata 198
fennel: fennel and lemon risotto 201

grilled vegetable pizza 174
shaved salad with toasted seeds 74
figs: beet and fig carpaccio 187
black fig jam 230
Camembert, watercress, and marinated figs 100
chocolate and fig granola 34
fig tapenade 240
frittata: oven-baked pea, barley, and fava bean 198
squash blossom and tomato 52
fritters, carrot 146
fruit 15
pickled fruit for cheese and salads 244
rich almond tart with red berry compote 228

G
garlic: garlic-herb butter 234
roasted garlic toasts 54
toasted garlic bread crumbs 104
see also wild garlic
gazpacho: gazpacho Andaluz 114
white gazpacho 116
ginger and lime dipping sauce 244
girolles: pan-fried girolles and sour cherries 220
globe artichokes: see artichokes
gnocchi: ricotta gnocchi gratin 176
goat cheese: pearl barley, mushrooms, and butternut squash 222
roasted red pepper and goat cheese bites 48
summer spring rolls 206
toasted goat cheese and charred tomato panini 30
a winter salad 78
gomashio 236
red cabbage slaw with 187
Gorgonzola sauce 240
grains 18
granola 34
grapes: white gazpacho 116
green tabbouleh 94
greens: greens dressed with walnut tarator 186
tamarind tempeh with sesame noodles and shredded greens 142
guacamole: guacamole salad 90
guacamole salsa 56
Gyngell, Skye 210

H
herbs 14
hollandaise, blender 240
honey and pumpkin seed granola 34
horseradish dressing 238
summer vegetable carpaccio with 144
hot and sour soup 110
hummus: carrot 54

Puy lentil 54
sprouted chickpea and avocado 60

J
jam, black fig 230
Japanese eggplant with miso 148
Jerusalem artichokes, braised, buttered chestnuts with 180

L
labne 50–1
warm salad of slow-roasted tomatoes, labne, and almonds 76
lasagne with many layers 196
leeks: pressed leek terrine 68
legumes 16, 92–93
Leigh, Rowley 214
lemon: citrus mayonnaise 192
giant couscous salad with preserved lemon 80
sweet lemon dressing 238
lentils: Puy lentil hummus, 54
tomato and spinach dhal 169
warm salad of slow-roasted tomatoes, labne, and almonds 76
lettuces: grilled Caesar salad 102
lime: ginger and lime dipping sauce 244
lime and chili butter 234

M
mangoes: mango and cashew smoothie 32
summer spring rolls 206
maple walnuts 104
mayonnaise 236
citrus mayonnaise 192
Dijon mayonnaise 68
Mazzei, Francesco 218
milk: blackberry milkshake 32
yogurt 36–37
minestrone, summer 120
miso, Japanese eggplant with 148
muesli, pear and walnut 26
muffins, chard and brie mini 40
mushrooms 14
beet and porcini broth 124
fine white lasagne 196
mushroom banh khoai 58
pan-fried girolles and sour cherries 220
pearl barley, mushrooms, and butternut squash 222
potsticker dumplings 44
quinoa with parsley pesto, cranberries, toasted hazelnuts, and mushrooms 88

N
nectarine and tomato salad 210
no-knead sourdough loaf 134
noodles, tamarind tempeh with sesame 142
nuts 17

Index

nut milk 28–29
sprouts 92–93

O

oats: almond milk and maple oatmeal 22
    pear and walnut muesli 26
    toasted honey and pumpkin seed
        granola 34
oils 17
    basil oil 210
okra: Vietnamese hot and sour soup 110
olives: fig tapenade 240
    olive and polenta cubes 105
    olive stromboli 132
    pissaladière 194
    robust caponata 46
    salad potato griddle cakes with 160
onions: baked red onions stuffed with
        toasted, spiced couscous 178
    pissaladière 194
orange, mozzarella, toasted sourdough,
    and radicchio salad 82
orecchiette pasta with broccoli and
    pine nuts 158
orzo: artichoke, orzo, and fava bean salad 86

P

pakoras, spring vegetable 66
pancakes: chervil pancakes with
        eggplant caviar 204
    mushroom banh khoai 58
    spinach, herb, and ricotta crêpes
        gratin 188
panelle 46
panzanella burrata 168
papaya: green papaya salad 186
Parmesan lace 105
parsley: charmoula dressing 244
    green tabbouleh 94
    parsley butter 234
    ricotta gnocchi gratin with parsley
        butter 176
    salsa verde dressing 238
parsnips: giant couscous salad 80
    parsnip and rosemary rolls 138
    parsnip, sage, and mascarpone
        risotto 172
pasta: artichoke, orzo, and fava
        bean salad 86
    borage tortelli with sage butter 218
    chili and crushed walnut rigatoni 166
    fine white lasagne 196
    orecchiette pasta with broccoli and
        pine nuts 158
    pumpkin and spinach rotolo 216
peanuts: satay sauce 244
pearl barley: grilled asparagus and warm
        pearl barley salad 96
    oven-baked pea, barley, and fava
        bean frittata 198

pearl barley, mushrooms, and butternut
    squash 222
pears: pear and Parmesan tarte tatin 224
    pear and walnut muesli 26
peas: oven-baked pea, barley, and fava
        bean frittata 198
    spring vegetable pakoras 66
Pemberton, Tom 222
peppers: gazpacho Andaluz 114
    giant couscous salad 80
    olive stromboli 132
    pepper compote 242
    roasted red pepper and goat cheese
        bites 48
    shopska salad 168
    sunblush terrine 62
pesto 238
    tomato and pesto risotto 200
pickled fruit for cheese and salads 244
pies: see tarts
pine nuts: orecchiette pasta with broccoli
        and 158
    pesto 238
pineapple: Vietnamese hot and sour
        soup 110
pissaladière 194
pistachio nuts: cherry and coconut
        granola 34
pizza: grilled vegetable pizza 174
    pizza bianca 136
polenta: olive and polenta cubes 105
pomegranate, chervil pancakes with 204
ponzu dipping sauce 70
porcini: beet and porcini broth 124
potatoes: cumin potato skins 56
    potato puree 220
    salad potato griddle cakes 160
potsticker dumplings 44
prunes: a winter salad 78
pulses, sprouts 92–3
pumpkin: pumpkin and spinach rotolo 216
    spiced pumpkin and feta puff pastry
        tarts 64
pumpkin seeds: toasted honey and
    pumpkin seed granola 34
Puy lentil hummus, 54

Q

quinoa with parsley pesto, cranberries,
    toasted hazelnuts, and mushrooms 88

R

radicchio: blood orange, mozzarella,
    toasted sourdough, and radicchio
    salad 82
radish: salad of avocado with white radish
    and carrot pickle, 84
raw vegetable and avocado soup 108
red cabbage slaw with gomashio 187
Reynaud, Stéphane 206

rice 18
    cashew fried rice 162
    warm salad of slow-roasted tomatoes,
        labne, and almonds 76
    see also risotto
ricotta: baked ricotta with avocado 24
    borage tortelli with sage butter 218
    pumpkin and spinach rotolo 216
    ricotta gnocchi gratin 176
    spinach, herb, and ricotta crêpes
        gratin 188
    sunblush terrine 62
rigatoni, chili and crushed walnut 166
risotto 200–1
    cauliflower pangrattato 201
    fennel and lemon risotto 201
    parsnip, sage, and mascarpone
        risotto 172
    risotto bianco 200
    tomato and pesto risotto 200
    wild garlic risotto 201
    zucchini and Taleggio risotto 200
rolls, parsnip and rosemary 138
root vegetable gratin 190

S

salads: artichoke, orzo, and fava
        bean salad 86
    beet and fig carpaccio 187
    blood orange, mozzarella, toasted
        sourdough, and radicchio salad 82
    Camembert, watercress, and marinated
        figs 100
    celery root rémoulade 152
    chana chaat 98
    giant couscous salad 80
    green papaya salad 186
    green tabbouleh 94
    grilled asparagus and warm pearl
        barley salad 96
    grilled Caesar salad 102
    guacamole salad 90
    nectarine and tomato salad 210
    quinoa with parsley pesto, cranberries,
        toasted hazelnuts, and mushrooms 88
    red cabbage slaw 187
    salad of avocado with white radish and
        carrot pickle 84
    shaved salad with toasted seeds 74
    shopska salad 168
    simple salad 168
    summer vegetable carpaccio 144
    toppings 104–5
    warm salad of slow-roasted tomatoes,
        labne, and almonds 76
    a winter salad 78
salsa 118
    guacamole salsa 56
    salsa verde dressing 238
sambal telur 184

satay sauce 244
sauces 240–4
   béchamel sauce 241
   best tomato sauce 241
   black vinegar dipping sauce 44
   blender hollandaise 240
   charmoula dressing 244
   chili tomato jam 242
   fig tapenade 240
   ginger and lime dipping sauce 244
   Gorgonzola sauce 240
   ponzu dipping sauce 70
   rustic, slow-roasted tomato sauce 242
   satay sauce 244
   soy dipping sauce 154
   tomato coulis 206
   walnut tarator 241
seeds 17
   seed milk 28–9
   sprouts 92–3
sesame seeds: gomashio 236
shaved salad with toasted seeds 74
shopska salad 168
side dishes 186–7
smoky black bean and roasted tomato
   soup 118
smoothie, mango and cashew 32
soda bread 130
soups 106–27
   beet and porcini broth 124
   butter bean and celery root velouté 126
   chilled cucumber and lovage soup 112
   gazpacho Andaluz 114
   raw vegetable and avocado soup 108
   smoky black bean and roasted tomato
      soup 118
   summer minestrone 120
   Vietnamese hot and sour soup 110
   white gazpacho 116
   winter squash and corn chowder 122
sourdough loaf, no-knead 134
soy milk: tofu 156–7
soy sauce: ponzu dipping sauce 70
   soy dipping sauce 154
soy sprouts: summer spring rolls 206
spinach: pumpkin and spinach rotolo 216
   spinach, herb, and ricotta crêpes
      gratin 188
   tomato and spinach dhal 169
spring rolls, summer 206
spring vegetable pakoras 66
sprouts 92–93
squash: see butternut squash; zucchini
   squash blossom and tomato frittatas 52
stock, vegetable 236
summer minestrone 120
summer spring rolls 206
summer vegetable carpaccio 144
sunblush terrine 62
sweet potato wedges 187

T
tabbouleh, green 94
tahini seeds 104
tamarind tempeh with sesame noodles 142
tapenade: beet and fig carpaccio
      with 187
   fig tapenade 240
tarts: cherry tomato tarte tatin 169
   pear and Parmesan tarte tatin 224
   pissaladière 194
   rich almond tart 228
   spiced pumpkin and feta puff pastry
      tarts 64
   tian of tomatoes and eggplant 214
   tomato and tarragon tart 169
tempeh, tamarind 142
tempura, mixed vegetable 70
terrines: pressed leek terrine 68
   sunblush terrine 62
tian of tomatoes and eggplant 214
toasts, roasted garlic 54
tofu 156–7
   crispy five-spice tofu with soy dipping
      sauce 154
tomatoes 168–9
   best tomato sauce 241
   cherry tomato tarte tatin 169
   chili tomato jam 242
   gazpacho Andaluz 114
   green tabbouleh topped with a cherry
      tomato salad 94
   nectarine and tomato salad 210
   panzanella burrata 168
   pissaladière 194
   rustic, slow-roasted tomato sauce 242
   shopska salad 168
   simple salad 168
   slow-roasted tomatoes 242
   smoky black bean and roasted tomato
      soup 118
   squash blossom and tomato frittatas 52
   sunblush terrine 62
   tian of tomatoes and eggplant 214
   toasted goat cheese and charred tomato
      panini 30
   tomato and pesto risotto 200
   tomato and spinach dhal 169
   tomato and tarragon tart 169
   tomato coulis 206
   warm salad of slow-roasted tomatoes,
      labne, and almonds 76
tortelli, borage 218
tortillas: guacamole salad 90

V
vegetables 15
   cashew fried rice 162
   mixed vegetable tempura 70
   shredded root vegetable gratin 190
   summer minestrone 120

summer vegetable carpaccio 144
   vegetable stock 236
Vietnamese hot and sour soup 110
vinegar: balsamic vinaigrette 236
   black vinegar dipping sauce 44
   pickled fruit for cheese and salads 244

W
walnuts: chili and crushed walnut
      rigatoni 166
   greens dressed with walnut
      tarator 186
   maple walnuts 104
   pear and walnut muesli 26
   walnut dressing 100
   walnut tarator 241
   a winter salad 78
watercress: Camembert, watercress, and
      marinated figs 100
white beans: grilled asparagus and warm
      pearl barley salad 96
white gazpacho 116
wild garlic risotto 201
a winter salad 78
winter squash and corn chowder 122
wonton wrappers, potsticker dumplings 44

Y
yogurt 19, 36–7
   blackberry milkshake 32
   chilled cucumber and lovage soup 112
   cucumber yogurt 42
   giant couscous salad 80
   labne 50–1
   toasted honey and pumpkin seed
      granola with 34

Z
zucchini: grilled vegetable pizza 174
   sunblush terrine 62
   zucchini and Taleggio risotto 200

Acknowledgments

Without the commission from, and vision of, Catie Ziller, this project would never have come to fruition. Thank you, Catie. Here's hoping it encourages everyone to cut back on the meat eating now and then.

Sue, your patience and serenity throughout the editing process have been astounding—thank you so much for all the extra words and help. Lisa, thank you for being so funny and kind day after day, and for not minding the chaos in your kitchen, in spite of which you managed to take particularly stunning pictures! Rashna, you have worked so inspiringly to create these beautiful pages and have never failed to be utterly charming and cheerful. And lovely Lou, who was a great help on shoot days, you are simply marvelous. What would we have done without you? Alice Chadwick has added such individuality and humor through her wonderful illustrations.

A special thank-you goes to Francesco for the bag of delicious goodies he sent to the shoot and to Petersham Nurseries for so kindly lending the beautiful zinc table (our "magic" table) that brought so many of the photographs in this book to life.

To chefs Stéphane, Skye, Rowley, Francesco, and Tom, thank you for so generously contributing your recipes. They have made the book even more special.

Stéphane Reynaud Villa9trois – 28, rue Colbert, 93100 Montreuil, France. Tel: +33 (0)1 48 58 17 37, www.villa9trois.com. **Skye Gyngell** Petersham Nurseries Cafe – Church Lane, Off Petersham Road, Richmond, TW10 7AG, England. Tel: +44 (0)208 605 3627, www.petershamnurseries.com. **Rowley Leigh** Le Café Anglais – 8 Porchester Gardens, London W2 4DB, England. Tel: +44 (0)20 7221 1415, www.lecafeanglais.co.uk. **Francesco Mazzei** L'Anima – 1 Snowden Street, Broadgate West, London EC2A 2DQ, England. Tel: +44 (0)207 422 7000, www.lanima.co.uk. **Tom Pemberton** Hereford Road Restaurant – 3 Hereford Road, Westbourne Grove, London W2 4AB, England. Tel: +44 (0)20 7727 1144, www.herefordroad.org

Lyons Press is an imprint of Globe Pequot Press
Library of Congress Cataloguing-in-Publication Data is available on file

ISBN: 978-0-7627-7897-3

Printed in China

10 9 8 7 6 5 4 3 2 1